Dear Me

Dear Me

A Letter to My Sixteen-Year-Old Self

Edited by

JOSEPH GALLIANO

ATRIA BOOKS

New York   London   Toronto   Sydney   New Delhi

ATRIA BOOKS
A Division of Simon & Schuster, Inc.
1230 Avenue of the Americas
New York, NY 10020

First Atria Books hardcover edition October 2011

ATRIA B O O K S and colophon are trademarks of Simon & Schuster, Inc.

For information about special discounts for bulk purchases, please contact Simon & Schuster Special Sales at 1-866-506-1949 or business@simonandschuster.com.

The Simon & Schuster Speakers Bureau can bring authors to your live event. For more information or to book an event, contact the Simon & Schuster Speakers Bureau at 1-866-248-3049 or visit our website at www.simonspeakers.com.

Designed by Kyoko Watanabe

Manufactured in the United States of America

10   9   8   7   6   5   4   3   2   1

Library of Congress Cataloging-in-Publication Data

Dear me : a letter to my sixteen-year-old self / edited by Joseph Galliano.
— 1st Atria books hardcover ed.
    p. cm.
1. Conduct of life. 2. Celebrities—Correspondence. I. Galliano, Joseph.
  BJ1581.2.D49 2011
  808.88'3—dc23   2011034911

ISBN 978-1-4516-4964-2
ISBN 978-1-4516-4968-0 (ebook)

Dedicated with love to dear friends
Nicholas Hull-Malham, 1951–2010,
and Kristian Digby, 1977–2010

FOREWORD
BY J. K. ROWLING

This is an extraordinary little book, based on a simple but wonderful idea: What would you say to yourself if you came face-to-face with the sixteen-year-old you?

One of the many things that delighted and touched me as I read the letters that follow is the commonality of our human experience. Nearly everyone who wrote, whether their letter is jolly or poignant, seems to have looked back on their younger selves with compassion, remembering how vulnerable and dangerous an age sixteen is, for all the fun and freedom it is supposed to entail.

The overwhelming message of this body of letters seems to be: Be yourself. Be easier on yourself. Become yourself, as fully as possible.

Attempting to isolate those life lessons I could pass back to the girl I used to be was a truly illuminating exercise. It made me look at my seventeen-year-old daughter and remember, in a more powerful way than ever before, just how raw and vivid life is for her, in a way that it has been only intermittently for me as an adult. I would not go back to sixteen for anything you could give me, and yet I still recognize that she has something I have lost along the way—something I had to lose, to stay sane.

You might have picked up this book out of interest in some of the fascinating people who have contributed. I don't think you will be disappointed. The great thing about these letters is that they are extraordinarily revealing, whether short, long, full of practical advice or metaphysical musings.

Whatever your motives in buying this book, thank you. One dollar a copy will benefit Doctors Without Borders.

Finally, let me urge you to use the blank pages at the end of the book to write your own letter to yourself, aged sixteen. I think you'll find it just as thought-provoking and worthwhile as we all did.

J. K. Rowling

INTRODUCTION

At age sixteen, I did a lot of staring out of windows—filled with terror, worrying about who I was or what I was going to be. Was I good, clever, hip, decent, fun enough? Was the world going to end? (This was the 1980s, after all, and the cold war was no joke.) Was I going to make it? I wore a troubled brow.

As we get older, some of our teenage intensity will ease, but when in the maelstrom, we don't know that. When we are young, we so rarely take the advice of grown-ups, but would you have taken advice from someone like you? From your older self perhaps?

My family have always been letter writers, and pens have always been precious to me. My mother's beautiful italicized script flowing from the left-handed gold nib of her Parker pen always struck me as the height of adult elegance. When, as a child, I would go away from home for any period, there would always be a long and comforting letter from her in my bag. And, of course, writing thank-you letters was as much a part of the holiday season as tinsel.

A few years ago my partner showed me a heartbreaking letter that he had received from a troubled classmate while he was still at school. It made me want to send a hug back in time to say, "You're okay, you're just fine."

But in reality, of course, that's impossible. (Time-travel mailbox in development anyone?) Instead, the "Dear Me" letter was born. Writing my own letter to myself and hearing what this experience has meant to this book's generous contributors has proven to me that composing a letter to your younger self is a cathartic process. The act of addressing yourself with kindness and adult understanding can give you a better sense of who you are now—for indeed, in many ways our childhood self is our parent. As Bob Dylan sang, "I was so much older then, I'm younger than that now."

Reading this collection is to be rewarded with an intimate glimpse into the backgrounds and emotional makeup of a wonderfully varied group of fascinating people, without the filter of the usual interview process.

I hope that you will smile, laugh, shed a tear, and take some comfort from these time-traveling missives and remember once again what it was like to be sixteen.

Joseph Galliano
London
June 19, 2011

CONTRIBUTOR BIOGRAPHIES

Hugh Jackman

This Australian star of film, musical theater, and TV is consistently voted one of the sexiest men alive.

Eileen Fulton

Played Lisa Grimaldi for fifty years on the soap opera *As The World Turns*.

John Waters

Director, writer, and stand-up comedian who rose to infamy in the 1970s for films such as *Pink Flamingos, Desperate Living*, and *Hairspray*. The Pope of Trash.

Jodi Picoult

Bestselling author of *My Sister's Keeper* and *Sing You Home*.

Lucas Cruikshank

Creator of Fred Figglehorn, the original YouTube star, and of the first YouTube channel to reach one million subscribers.

Cassandra Peterson

Elvira, Mistress of the Dark.

Bill T. Jones

Dancer, choreographer, and artistic director of the Bill T. Jones/Arnie Zane Dance Company, and a 2010 Kennedy Award winner.

Graydon Carter

Canadian-born editor of American magazine *Vanity Fair* since 1992.

Frank Luntz

American political consultant and pollster, commentator, and analyst.

Steve Vai

Ten-time Grammy nominee and three-time Grammy winner, whom Frank Zappa called his "Stunt Guitarist"; he has recorded and toured with Whitesnake, Public Image Ltd., and David Lee Roth.

Aasif Mandvi

Correspondent and Senior Egyptologist from *The Daily Show with Jon Stewart* who has also appeared in films such as *The Last Airbender* and *It's Kind of a Funny Story*.

Pattie Boyd

Photographer and model, the muse of former husbands George Harrison and Eric Clapton, and the inspiration behind some of the greatest love songs of the last century, including The Beatles' "Something" and Clapton's "Wonderful Tonight."

Kathleen Turner

American movie actress and star of *Peggy Sue Got Married*, *Body Heat*, and the voice of *Who Framed Roger Rabbit*'s Jessica Rabbit.

Greg Gorman

American portrait photographer whose work has appeared in *Vanity Fair*, *Vogue*, and *Rolling Stone*.

Stephen King

Novelist and undisputed King of Horror.

Beverly D'Angelo

Actress and singer who has appeared on *Law & Order: Special Victims Unit* and *Entourage* and is also beloved for playing Ellen Griswold in *National Lampoon's Vacation* and the country singer Lurleen Lumpkin in *The Simpsons*.

Alice Cooper

Much-loved heavy metal artist and bestselling author.

Dannii Minogue

Australian singer, songwriter, actress, media personality, fashion designer, model, and talent show judge.

Jon Lee Brody

Producer, director, writer, and star of the movies *The Science of Cool* and *Human Factor*.

Angie Dickinson

A fixture in film and on TV since 1954, she played the legendary sergeant Suzanne "Pepper" Anderson on 1970s TV series *Police Woman*.

Francisco Costa

Brazilian-born women's creative director for the Calvin Klein Collection.

Steve-O

Stunt performer and star of the Jackass TV series.

James Franco

Prolific actor, author, and artist who was nominated for an Academy Award for Best Actor for *127 Hours*.

Matthew Mitcham

Australian diver who won gold in the 2008 Beijing Olympics.

Ferran Adrià

The head chef of the famed Spanish restaurant El Bulli, holder of three Michelin stars.

Suze Orman

Emmy Award–winning television host and bestselling author, who was was twice named by *Time* as one of the World's 100 Most Influential People and named by *Forbes* as one of the World's 100 Most Powerful Women, she is America's most recognized expert on personal finance.

Chad Allen

Former child star, now actor and film producer best known for playing Matthew Cooper in *Dr. Quinn: Medicine Woman*.

Rita Rudner

American comedian, writer, actress, and Las Vegas institution.

James Woods

Academy Award nominee and multiple Emmy and Golden Globe–winning actor. Best known for roles in films like *Once Upon a Time in America, Nixon,* and *Salvador*.

George Watsky

Slam poet and rapper whose "Pale Kid Raps So Fast" YouTube video has had more than eleven million views.

Garth Brooks

The holder of two Grammys and sixteen American Music Awards, Garth is the bestselling solo artist of all time next to Elvis.

Melina Kanakaredes

Daytime Emmy Award–nominated actress, best known for her roles in *CSI: NY* and *Providence*.

Jessalyn Gilsig

Actress best known for playing Terri Schuester on *Glee*.

Armistead Maupin

Bestselling author of the *Tales of the City* novels.

David Arnold

English film soundtrack composer best known for his scores for the James Bond films, *Independence Day,* and *Zoolander*.

Gillian Anderson

Emmy and Golden Globe–winning actor best known for playing Special Agent Dana Scully on *The X-Files*.

J. K. Rowling

Author of the globally bestselling *Harry Potter* books.

James Avery

Emmy-winning actor best known for playing Philip Banks on *The Fresh Prince of Bel-Air*.

Sarah Ferguson, the Duchess of York
Charity patron, spokesperson, TV personality, film producer, and the author of several books, including *Finding Sarah*.

Gene Hackman
Star of classic films *The French Connection, The Poseidon Adventure, Get Shorty, Mississippi Burning,* and *The Royal Tenenbaums* who played Lex Luther in the *Superman* films.

Toby Jones
British actor who played Karl Rove in Oliver Stone's *W;* he is also the voice of Dobby in the *Harry Potter* movies.

Trischa Zorn-Hudson
The most decorated athlete in the history of the Paralympics, wining fifty-one medals between 1980 and 2004 for swimming, including forty-one Gold medals.

Mark Everett aka E from eels
Singer-songwriter (aka e) from the American rock band Eels.

Rose McGowan
Singer and actor who starred in *Charmed* and played two roles in Quentin Tarantino's *Grindhouse* double bill.

James Belushi
Film and TV actor and comedian who plays James "Jim" Orenthal on the sitcom *According to Jim.*

Alek Keshishian
Film director best known for *Madonna: Truth or Dare.*

Piers Morgan

Former British tabloid editor, TV presenter, memoirist, judge on *America's Got Talent,* winner of *Celebrity Apprentice,* and now the host of CNN's *Piers Morgan Tonight.*

Jenna Elfman

Golden Globe–winning actress who played Dharma on *Dharma and Greg.*

Stan Lee

Former president and chairman of Marvel Comics and cocreator of Spider-Man, Iron Man, The Fantastic Four, The X-Men, and many other comic-strip icons.

Seth Green

Actor, comedian, voice artist, and producer. The creator of the Robot Chicken animated series and the voice of *Family Guy*'s Chris Griffin.

Erykah Badu

Award-winning musician and actress known as "The First Lady of Neo Soul."

Dustin Lance Black

Academy Award–winning screenwriter of Gus Van Sant's *Milk.*

Moon Zappa

Actress, writer, singer, and daughter of iconic rock musician, composer, and satirist Frank Zappa.

Joseph Galliano

Journalist and originator and editor of this book.

Alan Rickman
Renowned British actor and theater director who also plays Severus Snape in the *Harry Potter* films.

Michael Winner
British restaurant critic and film director responsible for the Death Wish series.

Lynda Carter
The original Wonder Woman.

Paul Reubens
Star of film, stage, and the small screen as Pee-wee Herman.

Julie White
Plays Judy Witwicky in the Transformers film series and costarred as Nadine Swoboda in *Grace Under Fire*.

Pauly Shore
Actor and stand-up comedian who starred in *Encino Man* and the mockumentary *Pauly Shore Is Dead*.

Fred Schneider III
Front man of the B-52s and the Superions.

Jerry Springer
Former mayor of Cincinnati, Ohio, and host of the *Jerry Springer Show*.

Michelle Rodriguez
The star of films such as *Girlfight*, *Avatar*, *Resident Evil*, and *Battle: Los Angeles*, she also starred as Ana Lucia Cortez in TV's *Lost*.

James Marsters

Actor perhaps best known for playing Spike in *Buffy the Vampire Slayer* and *Angel*.

J. Alexander aka Miss J

Model, TV personality, and runway coach and judge on *America's Next Top Model*.

Phil Ramone

South African record producer behind worldwide hits from everyone from Stan Getz to Billy Joel to Elton John. Credited with recording Marilyn Monroe's "Happy Birthday, Mr. President" tribute to John F. Kennedy.

Neil LaBute

Acclaimed American playwright and film director of *The Company of Men*.

Ricki Lake

Talk show host, author, and actress who played the original Tracy Turnblad in John Waters's film *Hairspray*.

Alan Cumming

Scottish star of film, TV, and stage.

William Shatner

Captain James T. Kirk. What more need be said?

Jimmy Wales

Founder of Wikipedia.

Sandra Bernhard

Legendary stand-up comedian, actress, and singer.

Rob Thomas

Singer/songwriter from the massively popular band Matchbox Twenty and cowriter of Carlos Santana's mega hit "Smooth."

Zachary Gordon

Star of the hit film *Diary of a Wimpy Kid,* writing to his future sixteen-year-old self.

Mary Jo Frawley

One of Doctors Without Borders' most experienced aid workers. As a field nurse, Mary Jo has worked with medical teams to control infectious disease outbreaks such as Ebola, Marburg, malaria, and cholera; set up and ran feeding centers to deal with acute malnutrition; carried out measles vaccination programs; and worked in surgical, maternity, and pediatric wards. She has trained local nurses, midwives, and community health workers and spent fourteen months working in Haiti in the aftermath of the 2010 earthquake. Assignments have taken her to Ethiopia, Angola, the Democratic Republic of Congo, the Darfur region of Sudan, Liberia, Mexico, Nigeria, Pakistan, Sierra Leone, Somalia, Sri Lanka, Tajikistan, and Uganda.

Dear Me

HUGH JACKMAN

Dear Hugh,
Just thought I would pop you a little note to see how you are (even though I know) and to tell you that yes!!! There will come a time when you get over Penny dumping you at the bus stop. In fact you will see her in a couple of yrs and wonder why you cried every time you heard the Lionel Richie song "Penny Lover".

Oh and the patch of zits you get on your forehead will also go, but probably not as quickly as you hope. And Yes, you will get to move into the big room in the house as soon as your brother Ralph leaves.

Right now the important stuff is out of the way.....I will tell you a few things that may help you on the way. I don't want to spoil any surprises for you, so some of this may sound a little vague.

Things are going to be different from how you imagine them. I know you don't have a clear idea of what you are going to do with your life, and I know that drives you a little crazy... particularly as you get asked about it every other day of your life. But when you are asked just smile and say "no idea...but when I do know I'll get back to you".

Truth be told much of what is going to happen will surprise the pants off you... It will be way better than your wildest imaginings.

Love life? (spoiler alert) You will meet an incredible woman, and the choice to marry her will be the easiest choice of your life. Just listen to your gut. Keep writing down one list...and one list only... the 5 things you love to do, and the 5 things you are good at...they will keep changing, but one day they will match up...and there is your path...but even then keep writing your list just to make sure you are still on the right track.

Your nature is to be hard on your self... to push yourself... be careful of this... it can veer you off track faster than anything.

There is so much more to say, that would make you feel great to hear... but I don't want to spoil the surprise.

You have had many blessings in life, and will have many more... never forget where those blessings come from.

Oh... and in about 10 years there will be a hit song that you love called "wear sunscreen".....and a hell of a lot of it is true... particularly the bit about WEARING SUNSCREEN!!!! Hint hint.

I love you
From YOU!

P.S. buy shares in Google when they are invented!!!!!!

Eileen Fulton

Dear Very-young me,

Do _Not_ change your name. Margaret McLarty is a very good name. So what if people have trouble pronouncing it. They finally got Schwarzenegger- Zellweger & Bacharach right didn't they?

Please forget sunbathing. You will end up basting yourself like a turkey and smoking, it may make you feel sophisticated but it gives you bad breath- dingey teeth, and it is just plain dumb!

You do _Not_ have to marry the first man you sleep with. Do _NOT_ tolerate any abuse of any kind. You will be fine!

Love from a much older me, A.K.A Eileen Fulton, But still in my heart, Margaret McLarty ♡

JOHN WATERS

April 5, 2010

Dear John,

Be Angry now, like you ARE because when you get older it isn't so attractive. "Pissed off" at 16 is sexy, at 64 — its.... Spinning your wheels.

xx

John

To my sixteen-year-old self:

Since everyone is always telling you what's important in life, I'm going to tell you what isn't.

1. The backup plan that everyone tells you that you must have. You're supposed to have a safety net, because who on earth makes a living as a writer? You come from a long line of educators, and your mother will remind you that she has no intention of paying your rent once you graduate. A teaching degree — that's solid; that's bankable. She's right, and you'll even take her advice and get that piece of paper and write report cards for a hundred students. But getting a salary (one that works out to be $0.13 per hour when you figure in all the time you slave over the essays of middle school kids) is not the same as loving what you do. Find the thing that makes you leap out of bed in the morning, that's how badly you want to get to work. So few people in this world can say they love what they do. Isn't that a richness all its own?

2. That guy you cry over every night. You know which one: he broke your heart a thousand ways with one word, one glance? Twenty-five years from now he will call you and tell you that he's found your high school ring in the back of his desk drawer. You'll start talking and he will thank you for being the one constant in his adolescence, when his own family was falling apart. He

won't remember hurting you. But when you write, you will always remember what it felt like to have that bandage ripped off your heart. And that's why, when people read your stories, they'll bleed a little on the inside.

3. The fight you had with your mother this morning. It is hard to imagine that one day you will be exactly where she is, arguing with a sixteen-year-old. You'll learn to pick your battles. And you'll also learn to let go of the ones you think you will carry like a scar, forever. Over the years you'll have confidantes come and go, but your mom will always be your best friend.

4. Calculus. Trust me: you will never use it.

5. Your curls. One day the hair you fruitlessly tried to dominate with curling irons and blow dryers and Japanese straightening creams will finally take the upper hand and—are you sitting down?—you might even grow to love it a little. People will recognize you because of that mane of curls. It still gets

frizzy in damp weather, and you still want to tear it out sometimes . . . but one day you will be absolutely amazed (and a little disappointed) that none of your three children inherited it.

6. That you secretly think your brother is a total dork. He is four years younger than you and plays Dungeons & Dragons. But one day when you come home from college you will realize you missed the moment this ugly duckling got all swanned out—becoming funny and smart and entertaining. And what you will remember about your childhood is not how embarrassed you were by a kid who liked to wear Star Trek clothing, but the fact that when you ate Dixie ice cream cups, he always swapped you his chocolate for your vanilla.

7. The bump in your nose. You used to always wonder if everyone noticed it as much as you did. One day you are going to meet a guy who is so cute you cannot believe that he's talking to you, and you are going to become good friends. And then you're going to fall in love. And one day, when you get up the courage to ask him what he thinks of the bump in your nose he's going to say, "What bump?"

8. Being in a hurry. You want it all—college, love, success. The moment you realize you wish you hadn't grown up so fast is the moment it will be too late. So ditch your Type A personality and skip school one day. Go

on vacation but don't make any hotel reservation in advance. Take a class in something you know nothing about and don't think you're any good at. The scenery you see when you're driving in a car is completely different from the scenery you'd see if you walked the same stretch of road. In the car, you might see splashes of color; by foot, you'd realize they are butterflies.

9. Defrosting. You will not be able to remember a single day in your childhood when your mother did not defrost something to be cooked for dinner that night. Sometimes, because your dad was a picky eater, she even made multiple meals. When you get older you will wonder why you cannot seem to master this simple skill of planning a meal more than twelve minutes prior to cooking it. This, as it turns out, is not the important skill. What's more critical is being able to corral everyone who matters to you around a single table. You can be eating cereal or frozen pizza. It's not what you eat that is important, but instead what goes on between bites.

10. Where you came from. Okay, this one is sort of a lie. Where you came from *does* matter—but not nearly as much as where you are headed.

I'll be waiting for you.

XXOO

Jodi

Lucas Cruikshank

Dear Me,

Since being 16 was just last year, could you pass this letter on to me at 13?

Hey bud! How's middle school treating you? Yeah, you don't fit in all that well, but keep your head held high because you are about to be thrown on the most berserk and mind-blowing rollercoaster ride! You know how you've been casually making videos periodically and posting them online for the whole world to see? Well, those videos are about to take off, Lucas! I know it seems really nonsensical and unrealistic, but it's going to happen so you better keep on shoveling out those ideas in your brain, okay?

What's sad is that right now you're too frightened to even reveal to your closest friends your double life of being a chronic video-making buffoon. You're scared that they'll think it's weird that you're posting these random videos of yourself on the web. I guess it does sort of sound odd, like you're really attention-seeking or something, but trust me – YouTube is about to get exponentially bigger, so teens making videos is about to become the norm. And besides, they're all going to find out about your little "Fred" creation in a couple of months anyways, and guess what? They aren't totally creeped out over it; they actually think your erratic creations are funny. Although, I must say they're pretty perplexed that little awkward, coy-acting Lucas is portraying a hyperactive psycho in the videos.

Don't fret about the whole "shy thing" you're enduring right now. I mean, give yourself a break! You're 13...that's one of the most morbid years of a person's life. Obviously you're going to be a bit sheepish, I mean you're self-conscious about all the changes you're going through. I'll let you know that by your freshman year of high school you'll be back to your normal, somewhat out-going self again. The whole awkwardness thing is unfortunately going to stay with you for quite some time, but a dude that goes by the name of Michael Cera is about to hit the movie scene, which means that girls are going to start to find the whole "I lack social skills and can count how many friends I have on one hand" thing attractive. Maybe you should send Mr. Cera an advanced thank-you letter now for throwing lanky, shy boys on the map. I'm sure he'd appreciate it.

Lucas Cruikshank

Basically, just continue to be your complete and utter self despite what the flashy football-throwing boys in your grade say. I understand that right now you are renting your face out to a family of pimples, have teeth covered in wire, and face trouble daily when it comes to finding a place to sit in the cafeteria, but just keep on displaying your work for the world to see and it'll all just be a cringe-worthy memory before you know it.

Keep on having fun and remember, YOU created "Fred", so stay true to your vision!

PS: Your current science teacher is super hot, right? You can keep on pretending you don't understand the lessons she teaches so you can get one-on-one attention from her, but dude, wake up! She's married and is not attracted to males who are still venturing puberty.

Sincerely,

Lucas Cruikshank

May 11, 2011

Dear Sonia,

I have to admire you because you're one of the most independent, courageous and fearless girls I have ever known. Sometimes maybe a little too wild and reckless, but lucky for you, it works out.

Not many 16 year olds live on their own, go to high school and make a living dancing in bars at night!

When you make your mind up to do something, nothing can stop you. You're like a pit bull, a fighter that won't give up until you get what you want. In just one year you will have accomplished your "life's dream" of becoming a Las Vegas showgirl and then set out on new adventures.

The part I don't get is how you can do all that and have such incredibly low self-esteem.

Most of the time you feel ugly, worthless and unlovable. You spend way too much time staring at yourself in the mirror and only seeing the bad things, or at least what you perceive as bad. All you see are the scars from being burned. I've got to tell you that years later you'll return home and run into some of the people you hang out with now and most of them will tell you they don't remember you having scars!

ELVIRA
MISTRESS OF THE DARK

Joseph

But I know it doesn't matter if someone tells you that they don't notice your scars and that you're pretty. You wouldn't believe them anyway.

I only wish I could save you all the pain, tears and unhappiness you're going through now and will go through for so many years and through some magical time-warp message from the future, make you believe that you are beautiful and worthy of being loved.

XX

Cassandra

BILL T. JONES

Dear Bill T. aged 16,

First, let me say: You're going to be all right and I love you!

You should know that there are many people around you who think much higher of you than you think of yourself. Don't try so hard to impress people and be liked, but don't fall into a habit of yours, which is self-absorption and obsessing.

By now you are already sensing that you are not prone to organized systems of thought or behavior, but intuit your way thru everything. This is good, but I would encourage you to give yourself to the following list:

- Learn to speak a language or several. French & Spanish would be top of the list and Mandarin as well!
- Learn to read music and play an instrument. Piano would be great.
- Learn more about your African-American self in the context of world history.
- Don't be intimidated by Estella. She is your mother. She feels overwhelmed and very afraid.
- Find more time to spend with Gus even if he seems aloof. He is your father and he loves you.
- And finally, read Montaigne and remember his dictum: "Reflect on everything, regret nothing!"

In closing, you have always been loved and you have several great loves coming to accompany you in your journey.

Be brave,

Bill

Bill T. Jones

Arnie Zane

LOS ANGELES
6300 WILSHIRE BOULEVARD
LOS ANGELES, CA 90048
TEL: (323) 965-3400 • FAX: (323) 965-4952

LONDON
VOGUE HOUSE, 1 HANOVER SQUARE
LONDON, W1S 1JU, ENGLAND
TEL: 44-207-499-9080 • FAX: 44-207-460-6354

PARIS
4 PLACE DU PALAIS BOURBON
75007 PARIS
TEL: 331 44 11 78 52 • FAX: 331 45 51 89 80

VANITY FAIR

GRAYDON CARTER
EDITOR

Dear Me,

I send this along to you from many years hence.

First, let me dispense with all the obvious bits of advice: don't smoke, eat and drink in moderation, and exercise regularly.

And then:

A few things you'll always take with you: pen, paper, a good book, and a handkerchief (more on this later).

Always keep $20 tucked away in your wallet. You will be surprised how often it will come in handy.

If you do try drugs, dabble gently and briefly. Above all, don't make it a lifestyle.

Be hungry, but content.

Listen rather than talk.

A smile is better than a scowl.

Read constantly. And watch others every chance you get.

Be consistent without being predictable.

Bet on yourself. If you don't, how do you expect others to?

Treat your boss and those under you exactly the same.

Whatever you want to be doing in your 30s, you should be doing a version of it in your 20s. That is to say, if you want to be a magazine editor by your 40s, you should be well on your way to that goal by the end of your 30s. The same thing goes for your 50s, 60s and so forth.

Be decent.

CONDÉ NAST PUBLICATIONS

4 TIMES SQUARE, NEW YORK, NEW YORK 10036-6562 • DIRECT LINE: (212) 286-6397 • FAX: (212) 286-7728 • E MAIL: GCARTE@VF.COM

LOS ANGELES:
6300 WILSHIRE BOULEVARD
LOS ANGELES, CA 90048
TEL: (323) 965-3400 • FAX: (323) 965-4952

LONDON:
VOGUE HOUSE, 1 HANOVER SQUARE
LONDON, W1S 1JU, ENGLAND
TEL: 44-207-499-9080 • FAX: 44-207-460-6354

PARIS:
4 PLACE DU PALAIS BOURBON
75007 PARIS
TEL: 331 44 11 78 52 • FAX: 331 45 51 89 80

VANITY FAIR

GRAYDON CARTER
EDITOR

Life is not a dress rehearsal. But don't get hung up on every little thing. The key is to concentrate on the big issues and the little details. Everything in between will kind of take care of itself.

Stay open for business. There is no such thing as writer's block. Just start typing. At some point it will turn into writing.

Wish your friends well. It sounds simple, but it's the key to having a lot of them. Similarly, lose the people who you think don't wish you well.

Master the art of friendship maintenance.

Be comfortable with yourself. And I mean that two ways. Be comfortable with who you are. And be comfortable just being alone.

Get there on time. Arriving for a meeting or a meal five minutes ahead of time, gives you a period of relaxation. Arriving for a meeting or a meal five minutes late is not only stressful for you, but for the person you are to meet. And it means you do not have to begin every encounter by saying "I'm sorry..."

Partner well. Both at home and in business.

Go home at the end of the day. People with balance in their lives live better lives. Whether it's a family waiting for you, a partner, a dog, or just a good book, just go home. Don't make work your life. Make it your *day* life. Your evening life should be something completely different and even more fulfilling.

Relish time with your family. Invest in your spouse and children. Your returns will be exponential, rather than arithmetic.

Never hew too close to fashion. What with cameras everywhere, the photos will only come back to haunt you later. And will give your children endless opportunities for ridicule.

CONDÉ NAST PUBLICATIONS

4 TIMES SQUARE, NEW YORK, NEW YORK 10036-6562 • DIRECT LINE: (212) 286-6397 • FAX: (212) 286-7728 • E MAIL: GCARTE@VF.COM

LOS ANGELES:
6300 WILSHIRE BOULEVARD
LOS ANGELES, CA 90048
TEL: (323) 965-3400 • FAX: (323) 965-4952

LONDON:
VOGUE HOUSE, I HANOVER SQUARE
LONDON, WIS IJU, ENGLAND
TEL: 44-207-499-9080 • FAX: 44-207-460-6354

VANITY FAIR

GRAYDON CARTER
EDITOR

Always carry a handkerchief. Here are some, but certainly not all of its myriad uses:

- a) A bandage
- b) A napkin
- c) Something to wipe away tears during a breakup
- d) A sunhat
- e) When wetted, it can be used to cover your mouth during a fire
- f) A roadside emergency flag
- g) Something to write on
- h) Something to mop your brow in hot weather
- i) And when all fails, a surrender flag

Learn to juggle.

You don't learn a damn thing from successes, only failures. So don't fret about failures—just try to keep them small.

Invest early in those stocks with baby-speak names: Google, Apple, Yahoo!, and such.

Regarding the never-ending erection, the skinny wrists and ankles, and the hair so thick that your mother tells the barber to thin it out? Put them out of your mind. None of these will be long-term problems.

Lastly, the best things are to come. Call them Ash, Max, Spike, Bron, and Bella.

Love,

Older Me

New York, March 2011

CONDÉ NAST PUBLICATIONS
4 TIMES SQUARE, NEW YORK, NEW YORK 10036-6562 • DIRECT LINE: (212) 286-6397 • ___2) 286-7728 • E MAIL: GCARTE@VF.COM

To Frank Luntz — With every good wish & Very Best Regards.
Ronald Reagan

the word doctors
It's not what you say, it's what people hear.

Dude:

Lighten up...and shut up.

The most important piece of advice I can give you is that listening is so much more fun than talking. Nobody cares that you can say the presidents forwards and backwards in less than a minute or that you can name every state in alphabetical order. It was cute when you were ten. As you get older, it's going to get annoying. Please stop doing it -- NOW.

You're going to meet some really incredible people in the next few years, but you'll spend way to much time trying to impress them and way too little time trying to learn from them. Take that polling skill you're learning and apply it to your private life. Ask questions. The good news is that you'll eventually figure this out -- but not until you're 30.

Next, and this is just as important, you are way too young to have way too serious an outlook on life. The world isn't coming to an end, and neither is America. Stop arguing with every friend and every teacher about everything political. Nobody wants to hear your views -- you're a kid! It killed your social life in high school and it's going to damage it in college. I know you're going to learn this the hard way.

On a brighter note, all that student political stuff you do in college is going to train you well for your life in politics. You are about to discover some really incredible skills. Just don't let it consume you. Once again, you're going to learn the hard way that there's more to life than elections -- a lot more.

But I do have good news. In a few years, you're going to discover that being entertaining is a lot more conducive to a happy life. You're no comedian, and some of your "jokes" are going to get you into trouble, but you do have a skill for saying funny things. Use it. There's no reason to stand awkwardly in the corner at a party -- or leave early -- because you don't know anyone. Listen to the conversations and think of something funny to say. More often than not, it will get you into the conversation and you'll have a good time. Don't wait until you're middle-aged to figure this out.

Finally, some quick words of wisdom.

Eat that second piece of cake and have that extra scoop of ice cream. You're going to get fat, eventually, so eat everything you want while you still can.

Next, STOP BANGING YOUR HEAD AGAINST THE CONCRETE WALL whenever you get drunk. Yes, it gets you attention. Yes, it's going to get you invited to more keg parties. But it's going to kill a lot of brain cells you're going to need after you hit 40. Trust me. The social benefits at 18 aren't worth the health costs at 45.

And lastly, enjoy life as it happens. Live more for today. Spend more time hanging with your dad -- he's going to die sooner than you think and you're going to regret not being with him more. And listen more to your mom -- she's the wisest person you're ever going to meet, and she too will leave your life early. Appreciate the people around you. You're going to have an amazing life. Start enjoying it now.

May 2nd/2011.

Dear Asif.

I am writing to you from 30 yrs in the future & let me tell you something — You're a late bloomer! You always will be! Don't worry about it. Success. Sex. Money it will all come to you later than you expect it to', but it will come!

Right now, you have no idea who you are or what is going to happen, but you will be surprised at dreams you will fulfill.

Nothing in your life will happen the way you want it to, or think it will, but it will happen so don't stop dreaming and envisioning your future.

You have the ability to dream your life into reality so have the confidence to do it.

You have just moved from the U.K. to the U.S. and I know that you're lost, you feel foreign, you feel like an outsider, but guess what

It is that very fireyness, that outsiderness, that feeling of being "other" that is your power, and your mutability is the gift — use them both!

Keep Acting! It's what you're meant to do. Keep writing it's your salvation. Keep performing. It will keep you safe and happy.

As far as women go, I'm 45 and I'm still single, but there have been beautiful amazing women in my life, and even though right now you're a virgin — one day you will make love to some beautiful women — just wait!

Women are a mystery in many ways but they are part of your spiritual journey so learn from them, but don't let them define you! I don't think I should tell you to change what you are doing but I will tell you a couple of things that might help you.

Don't blow off your studies, try to get better grades and go to a better University. You won't, but hey, at least I told you.

Being best friends with a woman is NOT a way to get her to fall in love with you — Never works!

You're still gonna do it — but don't say I didn't warn you when you waste a lot of time and home your heart broken.

Stand still sometimes. Let life work itself out, it always does. Don't try too hard to be liked. Respect your own difference and trust your instincts. They're good!

Also, get your thyroid checked you are not supposed to be that skinny!

I love you man.
It's gonna be a good life

Aasif.

— Change your name to AASIF MANDVI
Trust me — It's better!

Pattie: second from right.

To a young me I would say:—
Walk, sit and stand with a straight back and always be True to, and love yourself.

Pattie Boyd

2400 East Missouri Avenue   Phoenix, AZ 85016   602.955.6600
For toll-free room reservations, call 800.950.0086
arizonabiltmore.com

Dear 16-year-old me,

I am writing to you from forty years passed by. I love your passion and confidence, and want to tell you that you are right. You are about to have your world destroyed; the safety and security you feel now, taken away. Know that you have been taught well, both in character and tools for learning. The lessons you have been given about love, loyalty, fairness, and determination will pay off. A few cautions: do not let your sense of humor, of the absurd, slip. Try to remember that what is happening at the moment is only that—a moment. Try the "count to five rule." Before reacting, before exploding, count to five.

You will be told that your dreams are absurd, childish fantasies. Don't believe anyone, however much they mean well. Trust that core that tells you your dreams are true. This is very hard because you have no way of knowing yet that they are, but rely on that darned stubbornness you are told is a fault.

Value loved ones and let them know you do. You will never be completely alone.

Give freely without considering the cost; it will never be too much.

Finally, love yourself. No one will be a harsher critic, so give yourself a break, OK?

Kathleen Turner

MARY KATHERINE TURNER "KATHY"
Springfield, Missouri
President 7; Editor of Newspaper;
Art; Drama; Madrigals;
Varsity —Volleyball; Softball;
Americanism Speech; Outspoken . . .
Extremely Intelligent
Forecast —Lady Ambassador To The Moon

GREG GORMAN

Dear Greg,

First off, I would recommend embracing your sexuality. Trust me, you aren't just going through a phase. Your straight friends, if they're truly your friends, will still like you. They'll probably like you more. You can't go through life worrying what someone is going to think of you simply because of who you sleep with. Actually, they're probably just jealous – enjoy your youth because your boyfriends will end up staying the same age but you are going to grow older, much older.

Always be true to yourself. Don't be a "yes" person in hopes of pleasing everyone. Trust me, you'll be the loser because you are compromising yourself. And remember you can never please everyone. You must please yourself first. That wisdom has come from living my life to the fullest with few regrets. Avoid reckless abandon but don't live the life others often wish to see you live. They aren't you! How can they know or even assume what gets your motor running at full speed!

Enjoy your life's journeys and when you've exhausted one journey, search out others and always keep your passion alive because that's what drives you. Your passion will always help you find your way. Loving what you do will keep you fresh and alert. Seeking new adventures will always keep you young, vibrant and most of all creative. Never believe your own press.

Diversify your friends. Having an eclectic mix of friends will certainly keep you in good form and more in touch with reality in this confusing and often frustrating city. Getting out and meeting people from all walks of life and all ages is really important. Be a good listener, something I sometimes tend to neglect. There's a lot to be learned and shared from other people. It really helps build lifetime relationships with friends that make a difference.

In closing, share your passions with others. Sharing for me has been the most rewarding part of my life on this planet. Age is really just a state of mind – a number. Funny that my age of 61 is just the reverse of 16, although with a lot more wisdom attached.

stephen king

Bangor, ME 04401

June 2010

Dear Me,

I'm writing to you from the year 2010, when I have reached the totally ridiculous age of sixty-two, in order to give you a piece of advice. It's simple, really, just five words: *stay away from recreational drugs.* You've got a lot of talent, and you're going to make lots of people happy with your stories, but—unfortunate but true—you are also a junkie waiting to happen. If you don't heed this letter and change the future, at least ten good years of your life—from age thirty to forty—are going to be a kind of dark eclipse where you disappoint a lot of people and fail to enjoy your own success. You will also come close to dying on several occasions. Do yourself a favor and enjoy a brighter, more productive world. Remember that, like love, resistance to temptation makes the heart grow stronger.

Stay clean.

Best regards,

BW— keeping a diary is a brilliant idea — and it makes it so easy to know exactly who you are, as I reach out to you from the future.... you say, at age 16, that you want "......gardenia tree walls, the music of angels or nothing at all" — although you are assuredly under the influence of that LSD you seem to love so much, this is still an EXCELLENT CHOICE.

You will have that and so much much more...

Six months from now, you will leave those cornfields and flat horizon for a world inconceivable to you at this moment. Don't worry, the angst you feel now is worth it. —Don't put so much value on happiness— it is overrated.... don't confuse lust with love, don't confuse experience with knowledge ..... true love will feel calm and wisdom will come from being true to yourself

take birth control and never start smoking accept everything offered from those who are what you want to become "DANCE" and do not a lot

DO NOT forget yourself

this girl ever

Sing every day no matter what

Trashy girls are exciting for about five minutes. . . . Keep your eye out for a really good-lookin' church girl. Then you'll have the best of both worlds.

PS: The Yardbirds rule.
PPS: I think coffee might really catch on, maybe call it Star something. . . .

Alice Cooper

Dannii Minogue

So...you are 16......

You live in Australia, have already worked for nine years in television and think it is a great hobby. I know you won't believe me, but you will still be working in entertainment when you are 40.

Singing and music will always be a part of your life, whether you are the one performing on stage or not. The phrase 'X Factor' will be a big part of your life and you will learn that mentoring is one of your favourite things.

All the hours learning to sew with your grandma will come in handy when you start up a fashion label with your best friend in London... oh yeah.... I forgot to say, you will move overseas in just three years.....even though you are not ready to leave home yet. There will be tears and sleepless nights and you will HATE the winter weather there. Buy some warmer clothing, because your Aussie wardrobe does not work in zero degrees. Brrrrvr.

You have and will always have the most eclectic circle of friends that you call, 'the circus', and that is just the way you like it. Most of them are creative or 'sparkly' and you will find yourself drawn to trying to get others to be open-minded.

ᴅᴍ

Dannii Minogue

You will get married and divorced at a young age.
The whole debacle will break your heart, but eventually
it will be a blip in the scheme of your life.

On a summer trip to Ibiza you will meet your true love
in a nightclub. I know ... tacky ... but you can never plan
these things! You have never been maternal or yearned for kids,
but you will just adore your baby boy. There is a light that
radiates from you whenever you see him or even think of him
.... and changing nappies is not as bad as you think.

Your family will never change. They are the same grounded,
loving people they have always been and they will get you
through ANYTHING.

Dannii x

PS. neon Bobbie socks are not cool and will never be back
in fashion. Deny, deny, deny, if you are asked about how
much hairspray you have used ... your teen hair do's may be
responsible for part of the hole in the ozone layer!

PPS. you are about to leave school for what you think is a
'break' but you will not go back. This is not a bad thing.
Learning how to touch type as an elective subject- will be the best
thing you learnt there- computers are gonna be big!

PPPS. you will meet your hero Olivia Newton-John and walk
across the desert with her in China singing 'magic'!

JON LEE BRODY

April 3, 2011

Dear Jon:

Well...I've seen 'Back to the Future' way too many times, and I know you have too so I think you'll understand when I say that I don't want to tell you too much because I wouldn't want you to change anything. Everything that you do is what makes me who I/we are today, and I'd like to think we're a hell of a guy.

I know it seems like mom and pop are just trying to make life difficult for you, but whatever they're telling you right now: they're right. They're always right. This is probably the toughest bit of information for you to fathom, but it's true. You may think they don't care about you, but they do more than you know. Mom is so hard on you because she knows you're meant for greater things and she doesn't want you to hold back.

Life is really short, dude, and before you know it pop's health wont be so great and you'll wish you had made more of an effort to get along with him. I know pop is rough around the edges, and he is stubborn as hell and difficult, but he loves you man and he really only wants what's best for you. Just remember that, especially when you guys have one of your many arguments.

I know you love your sports. And you're a stud athlete! Just remember there **are** things more important than football and basketball. Hard to believe, I know, but there's a whole world out there waiting for you. And sports are just a small part of it.

OK, I know having the drivers license is exciting but there's a cop hiding on one of the side streets when you're on Huntington, so be careful and just stay within the speed limit and you wont get that first speeding ticket.

And that girl you like so much and are trying to 'woo', don't get too down when she's not interested. Don't give up on being the 'nice guy'; being the 'bad boy' isn't what it's cracked up to be. You're better than that!

And most of all, just soak in every moment. Soak in high school and enjoy those years you'll have in college. Those are some of the best years of your life. Live in the moment, but don't forget there's a bright future ahead. No Regrets. There will be bumps in the road and they'll seem annoying but in actuality that's the good stuff.

And yes, Chris is and always will be the best friend we'll ever have! Oh and, yes, the acne will clear up I promise!

Lastly, dream big and never let anyone tell you that you should do otherwise. Impossible is Nothing! God gave you a great gift. So remember this: Your talent is God's gift to you, and what you do with it is your gift back to God. Don't stop believin', kid!

JLB

Dear Angie,

Treasure your abilities; you won't always have them.

"I can see. I can pee. I can hear.
I can bend. I can steer.
I can kneel. I can crawl.

I can run backwards.
I can chew.
I can do it all.
I can fall."

So, dear one, dance and ride your bike, but don't forget
that, one day, you won't be able to get back on.

Angie Dickinson

Francisco Costa

Calvin Klein Press Request

Publication: "Dear Me: A Letter to My Sixteen-Year-Old Self"

Country: US

Author name: Joseph Galliano

Questions for: Francisco Costa, Women's Creative Director, Calvin Klein Collection

Dear Francisco—

You don't know it yet, but you have only two more years before you ought to leave Brazil and move on to the next chapter of your life. The timing will be right for you to set out and pursue your interests in fashion and the arts—and there is no better place for you to begin this path than in New York City.

Yes, I know the idea of moving abroad and leaving your family behind seems quite daunting. You won't speak the language or have your close friends nearby to support you, but please don't give up on it. Just keep thinking of how exciting it will all be when you get to New York City.

Consider yourself lucky and embrace the challenges you will face with confidence and humor.

I can't promise it will be easy . . . you will have to work hard, study day and night, learn a new language, and forge your own path. But keep reassuring yourself that this is the journey you were meant to take, ever since you were a young boy and designed your first suit at age twelve. Make sure you hold on to and grow that passion—never stop learning and challenging yourself. Absorb the new culture and environment around you by immersing yourself and becoming a part of it, not by being a spectator, and eventually you will find your place. Sometimes, you have to go out on your own to see what you are able to achieve and fully realize your potential.

Love,

Francisco

Steve,

Twenty years from now you will be writing this letter to your 16-year-old self. Weird, I know, but here goes. You've just begun to experiment with drugs (and drink a lot of alcohol), and you also just started writing in a diary because you expect drugs and alcohol to negatively impact your memory from this point forward. I wonder why it is that you have such low standards and expectations for yourself. I'm not trying to be a dick, I just want you to think about that.

You live in a competitive world and skateboarding has taught you just about everything you need to know to survive. There's no such thing as becoming a good skateboarder without putting time and effort into it, and accepting that you're going to fall down and get hurt along the way. When you overcome your fears and do something you thought you'd never be capable of doing (that you really want to do), you're truly living. Incidentally, the skateboard introduced you to the video camera, and both of those things will help you more than you know! Don't ever worry about who's better than you, just stay focused on improving yourself. Overall, you are an incredibly lucky kid. I do believe that it's the hardest times you will go through that will benefit you the most, and that you will always be ok (even though you tend to believe the exact opposite). It sounds crazy to say, but I'm certain that you have angels watching over and protecting you, even arranging for you to have incredible opportunities. If there is anything that you are really likely to regret, it's that you didn't come to believe in your angels sooner. Believe in your angels, and don't be afraid to fail (not that that's ever been a terribly big problem for you!) You're a crazy kid, and that's ok — do what you've got to do, and remember to have fun. Life is about being happy. Ask yourself what happiness is, look for it in others, and find it for yourself.

Love,

Your 36-year-old self

Dear Matt,

Remember when you were young, all you ever wanted was to be special in some way – to be significant, to be remembered for something great after you died. You wanted to be the best in the world at something, and you latched onto sport to give yourself that chance to stand out. You would feel deflated, however, as you watched the Olympics and realised how unlikely it was that you were special enough for it to happen to you. Even when you started sliding into your dark years and had begun hating the sport, you persisted thinking it was your only chance to matter for something. Even when, for years, the direct cause of your profound depression was diving itself, you kept persisting. Guess what. It pays off.

Matthew Mitcham

DIVING GOLD
BEIJING 2008

Dear Ferran,

How are you? Well, I've called you Ferran, but really I should have written "Dear Fernando" or "Dear Nando." You live in 1978 and Franco has only been dead for three years; the Catalan language and Catalan names are only just reemerging from a long dark night that lasted nearly four decades. In your time you had to be called Fernando.

Spain is entering a new phase and is gradually catching up with the rest of Europe in terms of collective and individual freedoms, democratic culture, and the rights of its citizens. Now is when you realize all that you need! This is a unique opportunity. Will we seize it? Now is when you realize all that was missing! There will be a once-in-a-lifetime opportunity. Will we be able to exploit it?

It's been a long time since we last spoke, so I don't know what you do with your free time. Do you still like football as much? Do you still think Johan Cruyff is unique, the best? I know that your dream is to be the best, just like him. But let me tell you: do what you like the most, and take into account that spending 60 percent of your time asleep will not rid you of the need to work. Do you know what you will do in the future? I know you are studying business management. Persevere, because you can learn a lesson from everything, good and bad experiences alike.

But I imagine that you also still like going out, having fun with friends. . . . How's it going with girlfriends? It seems like it's still a bit of a chore; I know that you like girls, but at the moment you don't really feel like getting very involved. In short, there'll be enough time for all that, right?

By the way! I hope you already like lentils, now that you are at an age when you should try everything. I still remember when you locked yourself in the bathroom so that you wouldn't have to eat lentils. As I said, try everything. Your curiosity is what's going to allow you to grow and learn.

In short, Nando, I hope everything will go well in life. Take care and give a really big kiss from me to Mom, Dad, and your brother, Alberto.

A big hug,

Ferran Adrià

Ferran: bottom right.

Dear Suze   1967

I just wanted to write you this letter because I think
it is important for you to know that you really do not
need to be as sad as you currently are. I know you feel
as if everyone is smarter than you, that everyone is
prettier than you, and that everyone just has a better
life than you. But I want you to know that as you get
older you will come to find that none of that is true.
Your future is going to lead you to places that in a
million years you could never ever imagine. I don't
want to ruin the surprise, but let me tell you this.
You will never have to worry about finding love. You
will never have to worry about being able to support
yourself. You will never have to worry about who is
going to take care of your mom. You will never have
to worry about being happy or fulfilled. You will
accomplish far more than most. You will leave your
mark on this world in a way that no one else ever
has. Everyone will know your name. People you do
not even know will come up to you and tell you how
much they love you and thank you for changing their
lives. People will tell you that they wish they could
be you. People will look at you with total admiration
and respect. But most of all you will love your life. Not
just because of your accomplishments but because
you really really just love to wake up every morning
to see the sunrise. You will learn to always do what
is right versus what is easy. You will learn to always

stand in the truth. And you will learn that everything that happens in your life happens for the best. The only sad part is that your father does not live long enough to see what happens to his little girl. So love him up now, Suze, and be proud of who he has taught you to be. By the way, your mom will live to almost one hundred and the two of you will always take care of each other. Always remember, my dear Suze, to be as happy in your sadness as you are in your happiness and then you will know the key to life. Think great thoughts but always relish small treasures. Now stop wasting time being sad. Do you hear me.

Suze

08/09/10

mythgarden
"stories told"

Chad —
Stop Drinking!
O.K.... you'll deal
with that later, but
listen to me — you
have to know, you
are whole, perfect and
complete just as you
are! You don't have to
be afraid — you are
loved beyond imagining and
you will grow to find
and be loved so well you
won't believe it! (And he's
really cute too :)
You're going to help
a lot of people and do
really good work in the
world so relax, breath
deeply, look around — it's
its gonna go fast!
Say YES more!
and smile !!
Chad Allen, Love, Big Chad

RITMAR

Dear 16 year old Rita,

When you go to see The Who at Giants Stadium, bring a sweater.

Love,

[signature]

P.S. Be a comedian.

Las Vegas P&DC 89199
MON 21 MAR 2011 PM

AIR MAIL

JAMES WOODS

Dear Jimmy,

Don't change a thing really.

Just enjoy the fruits of life and take the hard knocks. One has no meaning without the other.

You have been blessed with a simple trick to make the best of life. It is a Woods family secret: treat everyone with respect and demand it of them as well. If someone abuses you more than once, you deserve it.

Call someone in your family every day of your life. You may think it is tedious to do so, but a time will come when you would give your life to make that call one more time.

Hug your mother often and tell her how much you love her.

Do good work and do it because it is a gift to the world. No matter how inconsequential others may feel about the value of your contribution, it is the giving that matters. The surprise here will be that the beneficiary who gains the most when you give is you.

Be proud, but humble. Be strong, but caring. Listen more than you may be inclined to do. Talk less.

And most importantly, call your brother on July 26, 2006, and tell him he must go to a different hospital.

It is okay to fall, but not okay to stay on the ground.

Cherish the dead you once loved so carelessly.

They still live in your heart.

James Woods

(2002)

DEAR GEORGE,

REMEMBER EARLIER TODAY AT SCHOOL WHEN YOU TOLD SARAH (YOUR FIRST KISS-LAST YEAR) THAT YOU LIKED HER, AND SHE SAID SHE WAS MORE INTO YOU AS A FRIEND? YEAH, I THOUGHT THAT MIGHT BE FRESH IN YOUR MIND. WELL, TONIGHT YOU'RE PROBABLY GOING TO TAKE OUT DAD'S OLD TYPEWRITER DURING THE THUNDERSTORM THAT'S HEADED DOWN THE COAST, AND YOU'RE GOING TO WRITE A PAINFULLY EMO✱ LETTER, THAT, MERCIFULLY, YOU WILL NEVER SEND. YOU WILL USE PHRASES LIKE, "I DIDN'T EXPECT YOUR LIPS TO BE SO SOFT," AND, "I GUESS I CAN'T REALLY SAY I LOVE YOU, BUT I LIKE YOU A WHOLE LOT." IT'S A LETTER THAT YOU WILL REFLECT ON 8 YEARS LATER WITH A MIX OF EMBARRASSMENT AND PRIDE. PRIDE BECAUSE THE INSTINCT THAT LED TO SUCH PAINFUL HONESTY WILL, ACTUALLY, EVENTUALLY BECOME YOUR CAREER ☺. THE REASON THAT ONLY THE LETTER TO SARAH SURVIVES ISN'T BECAUSE YOU ONLY WROTE ONE—IT'S BECAUSE YOU HAD THE BALLS TO ACTUALLY GIVE EVERY OTHER CRAPPY POEM AND OVERWROUGHT LETTER TO ITS INTENDED RECIPIENT. EMBARRASSMENT BECAUSE WE'RE SO CLUELESS. THE REASON SARAH WANTS TO STAY FRIENDS IS ① YOU'RE COMING ON WAY TOO STRONG, AND ② SHE'S SECRETLY DATING 6-FOOT LACROSSE STAR JONAH ▓▓▓▓▓▓▓▓. I HATE TO TELL YOU, BUT WE STILL HAVEN'T FIGURED OUT GIRLS COMPLETELY. BUT WHAT I CAN SAY IS WEATHER THE STORM. I KNOW EVERYTHING HAPPENING NOW SEEMS SO IMPORTANT, BUT THE FACT IS, THERE ARE ABOUT 7 BILLION PEOPLE ON THE PLANET (!) AND MOST OF THEM HAVE MORE SERIOUS ISSUES GOING ON IN THEIR LIVES THAN YOU. AND THAT DOESN'T MEAN YOUR PROBLEMS AREN'T REAL. THEY ARE, AND I KNOW BETTER THAN ANYONE HOW ROTTEN YOU FEEL RIGHT NOW. BUT YOUR LIFE IS AWESOME, EVEN IF MOM AND DAD ARE BEING JERKS ABOUT THE CAR. AND EVEN THOUGH SARAH WILL EVENTUALLY GO TO STANFORD, THEN MARRY A MOTORCYCLING FRENCHMAN NAMED OLIVIER, YOUR LIFE TURNS OUT PRETTY COOL TOO. LOVE, GEORGE (2011)

✱ EMO- adjective THE BELIEF THAT THE UNIQUE WORLD AND EXTRAORDINARY REVOLVES DESPAIR. AROUND YOU AND YOUR

Dear Sarah,

I've known you for a long time and you just said that you'd rather
just stay friends. I guess I deserved that after all the shit I put you through
in the past. Ever since I met you I knew that you were special. Every
time I drove under the tunner on the way to and from Marin I would hold my
breath and wish that you liked me. When I got your letter I was happy but
I didn;r know how to handle acceptance. I didn't call you but I felt really
guilty about it knowing I would regret it later. Sure enough, I did, so
when I met someone from Burkes and found out that you wrote the number
o n the letter wrong I was happy because I thought that there was a chance
that you'd still like me. Tht night when we kissed waa probably the best night
of my life to date. I di n't expe ct your lips to be so soft...I'm still not
sure why I didn't call you. I guess I felt like there was no way I could
duplicate that night. I've regretted that so many times...It's so awkward
at school noe. Not the same as before...and I had such hih expoectations.
I was really disapointed tonight but I have absolutely no reason to be angry
I wish I knew what the reason was but whatever reason you have is fair. I've
more than mathced any wrong that you could do to me. And not liking someone
isn;t even a wrong in the firs t pace. If there's nothing there beyong
friendship there for you then I can't change that, but it doasn't mean
I'm not going totry. I don't understand why we always have to talk about school
and the personal lives of your friends now though. We used to have such great
coversations...and how can you say I'm too nice? I thought being nice was
supposed to be a good thing. That's one of the things I like about you. I
like that yo 're loud. I like that you're short...I guess I can't say that
I love yo right now but I do like you a lot whatever happens. I hope that
things get better at school and it's not really awkward between us in the
play. I'm sorry for all the times I didn't make a move on you because I was
scared or whatever. I guess you'll probably never read this but I promise
if I ever get anotheer chance with you I;m going to make the most of it

George
November 2002

Hey pal . . .

I know this is going to sound crazy, but before you throw this letter away and think that I am a complete wacko, please, please, please read this letter in its entirety. I am writing us this letter on your fiftieth birthday, the year is 2012 (if you don't believe me just check the stamp and see that it costs a lot more than three cents to mail a letter these days . . .) and try to remember, hindsight is 20/20. The town you are growing up in is the PERFECT place to grow up. The college you will be attending is the very best you could ever ask for. There will be a friend from high school you will reunite with in college and that friend will save your life by saving your soul . . . please thank her for me. Speaking of girls, you have no idea how much what you say to a young girl will shape how she feels about herself. Things you never give a second thought will determine her level of self-respect and these "seeds" will last her entire lifetime. Girls at that age have no idea that boys will say things (sometimes very cruel things) to hide their own insecurities and immaturity. Please choose your words carefully, this is MOST important. "Why is this so important?" you ask, well, God has a tremendous sense of humor, pard . . . and He just may give you all girls as a parent . . . then you will know why. Finally, love your parents, enjoy high school, and have fun . . . oh, one more thing, your "across the street" neighbor is going to ask you to learn guitar with him . . . I suggest you take him up on it.

May God bless you and keep you, pal . . .

Garth Brooks

© Yukon Public Schools

1·6·11

Dear Melina,

It's been quite a few years since we thought, laughed, and lived in exactly the same moments... but your voice is still in my heart and mind. I think of you often, especially now that our daughters are getting older, although they are pretty far from 16. It seems that they have inherited a lot of our traits.

I'm certain you'd be surprised to know that some of those annoying things mom says and does, are things that you are now doing and saying. You know →

that weird way she teaches everyone to say our name... "Kan a ka ree deez, like can a wheeties." I know how embarassing it is, but it really comes in handy in the future. Trust me, everyone from your college professors to David Letterman will learn to say your name with that crazy connie analogy. By the way, "wheaties" really did come in a can when mom was young. One of your fans will send you an actual antique can in the near future.

Yeah, it's probably hard to believe now, because I know you aren't the coolest kid in high school... but you will actually have fans in the future. (and they won't all be related)

MELINA KANAKAREDES

actually the majority may be related :-)
keep dreaming, believing in yourself and
by all means keep practicing! The harder
you work the luckier you get... and
daddy's famous saying: "the only place
success comes before work is in the
dictionary"... always holds true.
Work is a tough subject for you right now.
working instead of football games, parties
and sleepovers is bringing you down
right now. You have to trust me
on this... working with your family,

no matter how embarassing the costumes
are, is exactly what makes you the
woman you become in the future. Selling
candy at festivals may be a bummer
right now... but as the years go by you
will realize that working with your family
and meeting hundreds of customers, will
define your future choices and values.
Those crazy times at the colonial, popcorn
fish and air show festivals, may actually
become a premise for a script or two
in your future.

FELIX DOOLITTLE

In closing I will tell you... just do what you're doing, try not to be so hard on mom, and enjoy every second of life. Although your path will have its twists and turns, you will get to do what you love (and get paid for it ☺)! Your work ethic and family will get you through the difficult times and our mom's way of growing older but *Never* growing up will become your way of life. You will turn out to be an extremely grateful and happy woman.

All my love,
Melina
(your older... *NOT* grown up self)

FD

FELIX DOOLITTLE

Dear 16 Year Old Self,

Look around. You have already met your ex-husband and father of your only child.

♥, J.

Dear Me,

Remember when you knew there was no turning back?

It was a muggy summer afternoon in Raleigh, and you had just dropped off your grandmother at the beauty parlor in the old Carolina Hotel on Nash Square. Killing time, you had wandered into the newsstand -- the "blind stand," as it was called back then, since it was run by a blind man -- and you and this sightless cashier were the only people in the room. There's no way he could have known where your eyes were fixed so feverishly, but you wondered if he was already on to you. What if his handicap had heightened his other senses? What if the mere sound of your footsteps had betrayed your exact location and the object of your lust?

You could easily have flipped through that magazine. Hell, you could have <u>bought</u> the damned thing. You could have told him it was Time or Field & Stream, and he would have been none the wiser. But you were so scared that you just left it there unexplored, fleeing the newsstand with a feeble "thank you, sir" to make it clear to him that you hadn't been shoplifting. It wasn't until you had reached the safety of your car (your <u>first</u> car, that Cherry Red VW) that you could let yourself reassemble the image that had so undone you. You had seen photos of shirtless men before — in the Sears catalog, for instance— but the guy on the cover of Demigods magazine, he of the oaken arms and golden chest, had not been there in the name of haberdashery; he'd been lolling in bed amid a tangle of silver satin sheets.

You turned on the car radio to collect yourself, only to hear a song called "Walk on the Wild Side," which seemed the perfect theme music for the moment, since it proclaimed with sultry trombones that you had already begun your long slide into hell. How could you argue with that? Apparently there were whole magazines out there devoted to your secret mental illness, or, as the state of North Carolina liked to put it, your "abominable crime against nature."

Okay, stop. Here's what I want you to know, son:

Forty years after that queasy epiphany you'll tell a
friend this story, and he'll smile knowingly. The next day
he'll come to your house with an old issue of Demigods --
not just any issue either, <u>the very one</u> — and you'll see
that your heartthrob had been just as beautiful as you
remembered (the arms, the chest, that rakish curl across
his forehead), though his name (Larry Kunz) will leave a
little something to be desired. As for those silver satin
sheets, they'll prove not to be sheets at all but a plastic
shower curtain wrapped around his waist. He's not even in
bed, in fact — that's a bathtub he's sitting on. Never
mind. He's all yours now, for as long as you want.

But you're wondering, of course, what you'll find
<u>inside</u> the magazine. Alas, no more photos of Mr. Kunz, but
lots of other young bucks with names like Troy Saxon and
Mike Nificent, decked out in posing straps and sailor caps.
You'll also appreciate the page of mail order gifts, exotic
items apparently indispensable to the manly household of
1962: An Indian pith helmet, an antique dealers' handbook,
a 21-inch imported Italian peppermill, a musical cigarette
box that played "Smoke Gets in Your Eyes."

And what will strike you most about this fading
artifact is how brazenly innocent it seems to you now.
You'll be hard pressed to recall how it had once filled you
with scorching shame, invoking that ominous war chant of a
word -- ho-mo-sex-u-al — you'd been trying so hard not
to hear. But you could never have known then that what you
feared most in yourself would one day become the source of
your greatest joy, the very foundation for your success.

Which is why, when Demigods finds its way back to you,
you will frame it and hang it on your kitchen wall. It
will stay there for years, a souvenir of bygone fears and a
source of daily amusement to you and the man you married.

Love,

Amistead

PS Nowadays kids can
call the Trevor Project for
the support you never received
866 4-U-TREVOR

Armistead: standing top right.

DAVID ARNOLD

APRIL 2011

Dear David,

Hello from the future. I'm writing this on the first piece of paper I could find. It's the kid's notepad - yes - you have three of them (kids, not notepads). Don't worry though, when they turn up you'll wonder why you waited so long to have them, its nothing to be scared of, although it can get scary. You'll realise why you're on the planet and you will simultaneously forgive your parents almost everything. The weird thing about all this is that you won't feel spectacularly different when you're older. You'll go through periods of loving things and hating things, trying to be someone you're not to see if that works - a million different pointless rebellions, but they will deliver you to a good place, so don't worry about what ANYBODY may have to say about it.

You know all that stuff you want to do? Well - you do end up doing it. It'll be really hard work but you know what you have to do. (You could probably get there a bit quicker if you don't waste quite so much time trying to figure out how to do it, rather than just doing it.)

The questions you have about people, the universe and everything will remain unanswered, but it won't matter because nothing makes sense anyway, and you will end up knowing who you are which renders all the other questions redundant anyway.

Love from me/you. David x

p.s. Don't be so scared of girls, they don't know anything you don't, they just make out that they do ..

Dear Gillian,

   You are completely and utterly self obsessed. If you spent a quarter of your time thinking about others instead of how much you hate your thighs, your level of contentment and self worth would expand exponentially. One thing I learned way too late in the game for my own good was that you can effectively increase your self esteem by doing estimable things. Therefore, I have signed you up to build homes for the homeless during your entire summer vacation. Your Christmas will be spent serving food at a battered women's shelter and Easter is designated to reading stories to children in the pediatric cancer ward. Four months out of 16 years dedicated to human beings other than yourself; you have gotten off easy. Oh and honey, expand your horizons; your world is a bigger oyster than your low self-esteem wants you to believe. Love yourself, think of others and be grateful. I love you, I believe in you, and I look forward to respecting you.

Me. You. Us.

P.S. Follow your dreams not your boyfriends.

JKR.Rip

Dear Jo (16),

I'm forty five. We're forty five! And, believe me, that is far from the strangest thing that has happened to us.

This must be a lot weirder for you than it is for me; after all, I know you. I also really like you, which you will find impossible to believe, given that you are racked with insecurity and self-loathing. Jo, give yourself a break. You're not the only one who feels small and inadequate; you'll realise eventually that everyone is the wizard of Oz. Time spent dreading and regretting really is time wasted (whereas time spent daydreaming, inventing words and writing stories is time very well spent. Keep that up.)

There's so much I could say to try and prepare you for what I know is coming, both the wonderful and the not-so-wonderful. The trouble is that the more I think about it, the more I realise that you need to just plough straight ahead and make all the big mistakes, because out of them will come some of your greatest blessings. Just know that there has never yet been a situation so awful that we haven't been able to wring some good out of it (and that is about the proudest statement I've ever made in my - sorry, our - life.) Everything you most want will come to you; some of what you most fear will also happen, but the world will keep turning, and you will be fine.

A few pieces of advice that I think I can give, without upsetting the cosmic balance:

- Bright red, baggy dungarees from Miss Selfridge will be a bad idea, even in 1983.
- White-blonde hair, while a fantastic look on Debbie Harry, will not work on you.
- Do not have your ears pierced by a hippy at a music festival. That was one nasty infection.
- Never bother trying to impress anyone who thinks that other people ought to try and impress them.
- Stop smoking NOW.
- Stick up for yourself a bit more.
- Forgive yourself a lot more.
- Avoid bass players. All of them.

In a year's time, one of the best friends of your life will arrive in that porta-cabin they use for the sixth form. You will know him by his Ford Anglia, his love of Elvis and his ability to make you laugh until you are unable to breathe. You might want to persuade him to hang onto the car. It could come in handy for, say, a film.

Never cut short a 'phone call with your mother. Never forget to say 'I love you.'

One last thing.

One day, you will not only meet Morrissey, but *he will know who you are.*

I KNOW!

With lots of love,

Jo (45) X △ X

One day, that will make sense to you.

hey you,

what a trip to be able to talk to "me" at 16...there's so much I'd like to tell you, but the world you're going into should be new. I know about Kennedy's assassination and the other stuff you've experienced; civil rights and what not...but guess what? we have a black president...I know you never thought it would happen, but it did...so it makes everything your mom said about you being anything you wanted to be true.

I just want to tell you that the world is bigger than the jersey shore...and the possibilities for your life are endless...so enjoy being sixteen, it won't come again.

OH...stop trying to understand "camus" you'll get it later...all the best

By KIND HAND.
———— II ———— .

Joseph GALLIANO. Esq.,

———— II ————

S.

2010

Dearest Sarah,

I am so full of admiration to you, dearest Girl, for all your honesty and for knowing your feelings. You must have a huge anxiety at leaving your school, and your friends and actually even your home life. You are like a pioneer lady... branching out to new horizons - to pastures new. Wow, you really are brave and courageous. Take a moment and be gentle with your little Sarah. You are going to have to take mini steps. I always say to myself that if I get through to lunchtime, without losing my marbles or throwing my toys out of my pram,!! then I have done well. I look at Nature, and see the trees changing, the leaves going from so many different colours. I always think the seasons come and go, the clock chimes, the minutes pass by. The sun comes up in the morning, and dusk welcomes the darkness, to cool the earth. So, Sarah my friend, whatever you do going forward - go with the sense of security, that you are embraced and nurtured and deeply loved. I know you have a sense of loss from leaving school, but with new horizons comes opportunities.

and for you Sarah, I think it is really important you go to spend time with your Mother. You have not really seen her properly for 4 years, since the divorce, and at 16, I believe a mothers' love is crucial, and especially for you. It has been tough enough for you. You have felt so lonely and that the divorce was your fault. It was not. You are a special and golden hearted beautiful red head, with a magical figure, and a father and sister that adore you - and a mother who is waiting for you. Please don't feel alone. Please don't judge yourself so Harshly.... Nobody

in your life, except me, understands what a monster judge you are to yourself. I want to give you permission to know that you are safe and loved. You Are not alone. You have done nothing wrong. I know you think that you are stupid, and that you have failed yourself, your parents, and you did not go to the same boarding school as your other friends, so you thought you were stupid and had failed. I am here to tell you, you did not, you are a star. You have done nothing wrong ...

13...

Every day without a structure and without direction. I am not going to University - I actually don't think I worked hard enough or got the grades!! Another telling off from Dads!! So - September AAAgh - it will come so quickly, and I'm off to live with Mum for a few months.... She has some cute looking english boys staying with her, working on the Farm, learning to play polo..... Anyway more news later! I will send you a postcard or 100!

lots of love ~ Sarah, aged 16!

P.S. Please can you give me any advice?

Gene--

Hey, daddy-o, what's up. Hear you been hanging out at the post office talking to those jarhead recruiters about joining up. The Marines are a great outfit but there's plenty of time, plowboy. Finish school first.

What's with mom talking to you after the picture show about Errol Flynn and acting? What do you think? In any case, if you decide to be an actor, you'd probably be banned from the neighborhood.

Coach Ave at school might be worth listening to. His advice about Hemingway, reading the classics, and applying oneself could be beneficial.

If you did decide to take up acting, maybe you should think about New York instead of Hollywood. It might be easier. Ha ha.

All the best. Remember, there ain't no yellow brick road out there.

--The Wizard.

Toby Jones

Dear 16 year old Toby,

I'm very glad to have this opportunity to write to you. You are often in my thoughts. In fact I know that I think about you far more than you ever thought about me. You are far more of an influence on my daily life than you could have possibly predicted.

I know its embarassing but I've always assumed that we're actually quite similar to each other. Yes I still love the music, the books, the movies, the banter we swore we'd always love. Some things have changed. I have imagined your disappointment sometimes at certain forks in our road. I can hear you logging the compromises - disgusted by my political inertia, sighing when I leave the party too early. I confess that some of these decisions have been more predictable than you used to promise they would be.

I talk much less than you used to: less and less with each year that separates us. But I also think I've become a little less serious than you or maybe just a little less preoccupied with proving my seriousness.

Don't worry about being right all the time. Just keep on enjoying the careless, obsessive, lustful, covert, insidious, illicit, idiotic, secret intensity of the epic you're living through. I'll sort it all out later! I know they keep telling you sixteen lasts a year but it still feels way longer than that.

You'll have spotted my waffle. No advice. I could tell you to learn an instrument but I know for a fact you'll nod, slope off and never get round to it.

Thank you for everything you're doing for me —

P.S. Make sure you see the Clash. There isn't much time.
P.P.S. I actually met Bruce Springsteen.

Fishers, Indiana 2011

Dear T,

You have not realized it yet, but you are just beginning and will have the opportunity to experience different cultures and go places in the world where others have not yet been.

Your dedication, determination and drive to prove others wrong about your abilities - rather than your visual disability - will definitely take you a long way in life. Although there will be peeks and valleys throughout your life, like on a rollercoaster, your constant competitiveness and eagerness to succeed will carry you through to the end.

Although you are now in a phase where others' ignorance of visual disabilities leads to them calling you names and poking fun at your disability, you will eventually touch, impact and make a difference to so many lives.

Breaking barriers and social stigmas about people with physical disabilities will be one of your strong characteristics.

Due to your hard work and determination you will become the first physically disabled Division I collegiate athlete to earn a full athletic scholarship for swimming, at the University of Nebraska-Lincoln. Again, breaking barriers and being an over-achiever means you will go on to earn All American and All Academic status for college sports; something that no one else has achieved as yet.

You will eventually be approached by strangers to compete in your first Paralympic Games (Olympic style event for those with physical disabilities held two weeks after the Olympic Games) in Arnham, Holland. At this point in your life you have no idea what the Paralympics are, or what to expect. Due to your infectious curiosity you will agree to participate in the 1980 Paralympic Games. This will have a life long impact both from an athletic standpoint - by becoming the most decorated Paralympic athlete in history with 41 Gold, 9 Silver, and 5 Bronze medals while competing in 7 Paralympic Games - to your personal life, where you will meet and become friends for twenty years before eventually marrying your future husband and soul mate.

Having a family that is supportive of your athletic and educational goals is very important to you. Make sure you cherish every moment with them like it is your last. You know your Mother is your biggest advocate and cheerleader, driving you to all your workouts and going to all of your swim meets locally and overseas. Unfortunately, while you are training hard for your last competition, at the Paralympic Games in Athens, Greece, your Mom will become ill with cancer and pass away three months before she is supposed to see you compete for the final time. Staying strong and NOT giving up during this difficult time in your life means you will choose to compete and can dedicate your final swim and medal to the memory of your Mom.

You will realize through this experience that medals and awards are not everything, but rather that the memory each medal or award represents is irreplaceable.

You are a person that likes surprises and there will be plenty for you to enjoy or forgive during your ride on the rollercoaster of life. You will be blessed with a lot of love and laughter in your life as well.

You are going to receive and give more love than your arms can ever hold.

You are an innocent and shy, but determined young lady who is always surprising people with her determination and fearless personality by trying and doing anything to prove to people that anything is possible if you only make the attempt.

Continue to live life to the fullest. Remember, there will be bumps in the road along the way. It is how you respond and how you handle these obstacles and what you learn from them that matters the most.

I love you and am looking out for your best interests.

Continue to be kind and compassionate to those lives you touch along the way.

Love & God Bless,

Trischa

Trischa (age 46)

MARK EVERETT aka E FROM EELS

Chateau E
June 12, 2010

Dear sweet, naive, 16 year old me,

You poor sap. I know you won't believe any of this, but you should.
How can I get it through your thick, acne-pocked skull? All the stupid things you are so worried about really aren't very important at
all. In fact, they are the opposite of important. What if I told you
that all the "winners" around you right now were actually the losers?
Well, I just did tell you that, but you still don't believe me because
I'm an adult and 16 year olds can never trust adults.

What if I tried to explain it this way: That feeling that you've never
been able to put a name on -- it feels something like, let's say, a
bone-crushing insecurity and cluelessness about your place in the
world -- just forget about it! That's right. You can forget about it
and go about your days -- confident with the knowledge that it's all
going to work out just fine. Because as you get older, you will figure
stuff out. A lot of stuff. And that bone-crushing feeling will slowly
dissipate. I'm sorry. I can't remember if you knew what the word 'dissipate' meant when you were 16. You will feel it less and less as
time goes on. That's what I meant to say.

And all those "winners" who appear to be at the top of their games
and lives are indeed, just that: at their peaks! It's all downhill
for those idiots from here. Ha! Come on, let's have a laugh. At their
expense! It's okay. You've earned it!

While YOU get to do the opposite: Things will just get better and
better for you. And here's the best part: It turns out that girls
like geeky smart guys much more than dumb sports guys. For many reasons.
You'll see. So relax, man. Just relax. And I can even pass along this
shocking piece of information: You will even enjoy your life in your
40s! You heard me. It's gonna be great!

Now, I'm not saying it's not going to come with some serious bumps in the road
along the way, but don't worry. Those bumps are the very thing that
will make you a better person along the way and make you appreciate
yourself and the world around you more and more. So you can stop marxing
worrying about the mean kids around you and stop putting any energy
into being mean yourself. Ignore all that crap and enjoy the nice things
in your life. Now how 'bout a smile? No? Well, you ARE 16, I get it.
But I can tell you're smiling just a little on the inside.

Sincerely,

E

A Fully Grown Man Called E

eels

To: **ROSE0905@aol.com**
From: **RM@RoseMcGowan.com**
Subject:

Dear Version 1.0,

There you are, a spitfire in your uniform of black Doc Marten boots, black tights, black miniskirt, white boy's button-down shirt, and your Revlon Love That Red lipstick. You keep the world and people at bay with rapid-fire delivery of some very tart words. In your mind, avoidance of closeness means avoidance of pain.

You are right to be afraid of pain. In your future there will be tremendous loss and some rough, rough sailing ahead. However, you are *not* right in thinking the pain will blow you away like so much dust.

You're a fighter, always have been. One of your curses is that people will see your exterior and assume you're tougher than you are. Everyone gets dealt some cards, that's one of yours. I wish you knew how much strength lies in simply saying that your feelings are hurt. Revealing your sensitivities is actually a very powerful thing.

Along the way you will meet artists and statesmen, you'll travel and work in far-flung places to do far-flung things. But then you've always known that. Deep down. Keep listening to that inner voice. It will carry you. It carries you still.

Sent from my iPad1

James Belushi

Dear Sixteen-Year-Old Jimmy,

I know you're sitting in County Jail right now for the next three days because Judge Nolan was sick of seeing you in Juvenile Court. You're feeling alone (with creepy people staring at you), hopeless, worthless and bitter over "something you didn't do"... but we both know you did it, Jimmy. It's okay, you didn't hurt anybody. It was a victimless crime. Just punk stuff. I know you feel like the victim. If you just got more attention, you wouldn't have to go to these lengths to be seen.

You really don't know the difference between positive and negative attention, do you? I know that even though your parents and your family treat you like you don't exist, football doesn't ever bring positive enough attention because you don't ever get to carry the damn ball, wrestling doesn't get you enough attention because they make the big seniors wrestle you and they pin you all the time, you always feel too stupid and not well-read enough to talk in class, you're a little dyslexic, and even in the pool hall you are a lousy shot, but Jimmy, listen to me: you DO exist. And everybody will know you exist after you play Luther Billis in your high school production of South Pacific. That will begin your turnaround. You won't have to get in trouble any more to get attention—and you will finally get the positive attention that you so desperately need.

Trust me, even in this moment when you hate yourself and want to disappear, you will be able to mine these feelings in your career in the not so distant future. You will have great mentors in the next four years. Richard Holgate at College of DuPage will guide you through your initial steps towards major changes in your life. Things will look better from the balcony of the Hotel Du Cap in St. Antibes during your first European movie premiere. And I don't know what to tell you about women except for that they can be very beautiful-VERY fun- but you don't have to marry every one you sleep with. It gets costly.

Good luck,

Future Jim

ALEK KESHISHIAN

Dear Alek
Relax.
Love,
   Alek xx

Alek: third from left.

Dear Piers,

Always heed the following advice from family and mentors:

1) From your grandmother Margot: 'One day you're the cock of the walk, the next a feather duster.'
2) From your mother Gabrielle: 'Ambition knows no bounds.'
3) From your father Glynne: 'Always be nice to policemen, and drink the finest French wine you can afford.'
4) From your army colonel brother Jeremy: 'Remember the 7 'Ps' – prior planning and preparation prevents piss-poor performance.'
5) From Kelvin MacKenzie, legendary former Sun newspaperman: 'Never edit on a hangover, and always get out of trouble a million miles an hour.'
6) From Donald Trump: 'Think big and kick ass.'
7) From Rupert Murdoch: 'Stiffs don't sell papers.'
8) From Simon Cowell: 'Treat everyone who works for you as if they have a badge on their head saying: Make me feel important today.'
9) From John Ferriter, your manager: 'No is not an option.'
10) From your older self: 'Don't take anything too seriously.'

Kind regards

PIERS MORGAN

Jenna Elfman

Dear 16-year old Me,

I just want you to know:

1.) Your first instinct is always right.

2.) Don't take people's occasional rudeness personally. It's usually their insecurity or hormones. Or both. Or they're just ignorant and have a low IQ. Or they are just human and having the occasional "bad day" just like you do sometimes.

3.) No one has the right to tell you what you should do with your life. It's YOUR life. You don't have to answer to ANYBODY—At least with regard to your personal goals. Curfew until your age 18 is legitimately your parents' domain. Sorry.)

4.) Your mom and dad aren't actually idiots, as it turns out.

5.) You'll thank your mom later. No really, you will. I promise. You'll see...

6.) Everyone else is just as confused as you are. Or more. Probably.

7.) Those "cool" girls that you are jealous of and intimidated by, who treat you like shit—turns out they are depressed losers now, so don't worry about it.

8.) All that spunk and energy that a few people tried to squash—turns out that's the exact stuff that will make you special and successful. Don't let them squash it.

9.) I know that wearing the braces and headgear from 6th thru 9th grade is absolute torture, but having straight teeth is awesome.

10.) You are a good girl. Don't be too hard on yourself. You're great.

Much love,

Jenna

Dear Stan,

I still remember how you always wanted to be a writer. In your last year at De Witt Clinton High School you practiced signing your name, Stanley Martin Lieber, over and over again, making it look as bold and impressive as any of those at the bottom of the Declaration of Independence. You were certain the day would come when you'd write the Great American Novel and people would ask for your autograph and you wanted to be prepared.

How could you have imagined the ironic development in later years? Today, people do occasionally request your autograph, but not for the Great American Novel which you never wrote, but rather for the oh-so-oft-maligned comic books which nobody ever respected years ago. And, even more ironic, the name you now sign is Stan Lee, which you adopted legally because you were embarrassed that Stanley M. Lieber was writing those lowly comics-- which have since become the wellspring for respected motion pictures, TV series, video games and all sorts of enormously popular globe-spanning entertainment.

So bear this in mind, my impulsive 16-year old self-- nothing ever stays the same. Tastes change and the culture changes. The important thing is to stay on top of what is au courant and be resilient enough to go with the flow and change with the tide.

And, if you're lucky enough to be one who contributes to the change in culture, never forget your roots or those who helped you make the grade.

Excelsior!

You

Stan Lee

(Stan Lee)

SETH GREEN

Hi Seth,

Let's start with that- I know you've taken an enormous amount of crap for the funny name up to this point, but let me assure you in just 10 years, your name will be crazy common. Seriously, I know it's improbable, but even successful famous people will be named Seth. Like you'll be in a room and someone will say 'Seth' and a BUNCH of people will say 'yes?' So stop hating your parents for the handicap.

Let me just say this- it gets easier. I know right now it sucks, family unit dissolving, personal identity in crisis, constant reminders that you don't belong where you are- but it gets easier. Hard work pays off, and you will find people and places that allow and encourage you to be the best YOU that you can, so seek them out.

Plus you get much less awkward. You will literally wake up one day and realize you don't have to impress anyone to have them to like you. Don't try so hard, and things will get easier.

Don't quit. Don't leave any vision unrealized. Believe in yourself. Actually, I can't stress that enough- no one will believe in you if you don't truly believe in yourself. So work through all the self-doubt and self-loathing and get down to business. You will work for at least the next 30 years, each year harder than the last. I know that doesn't sound so great, but you will make lots of your own stuff and work closely with almost every one of your heroes and they will enjoy it, so...that takes the sting out, right?

Last thing, you have to stop wearing what you're wearing. I know you're 'making statements' and 'challenging stereotypes' but you are trying a little too hard and just a little misguided. Plus in the future, there's a magic device that links every piece of recorded media together in a way that can be viewed by anyone, anywhere forever and ever. So that commercial you did when you were 7 where you look really stupid, and that sweet summer camp photo from 1982 where you're in shorts and really sunburned? Those will be available into perpetuity, so be careful what you put out there.

Aside from that, it's up to you. Everything that you don't get, everything that you suffer through- all your mistakes and triumphs get you exactly where you need to be. Enjoy the adventure.

Much love,

Seth

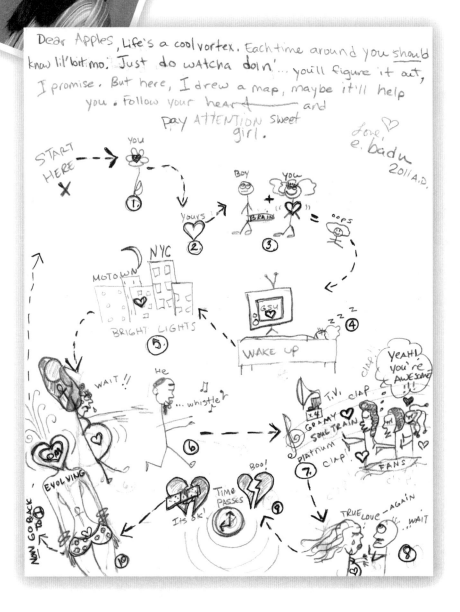

Happy 16th Birthday Lancer,

First and foremost, this means that in two days, as you're waiting for your mom to pick you up and take you to your DMV driver's test, Jeremy from your swim team is going to try and kiss you. Let him! You'll regret it the rest of your life if you don't.

Nearly as important, I know you had your first crush on a boy at 6 years old and that you've hidden those feelings for almost a decade now. That hiding has turned you painfully shy, kept you from excelling so you don't stick out, and on more nights than not you go to sleep pushing back tears, feeling unworthy, unloved and unholy. Worse still, I know why you hide -- you're deathly afraid you'll be hurt if you don't.

Unfortunately, your fears are well founded. The one "Health and Human Sexuality" teacher in your school condemns gay people. Gangs run the halls, students are beaten and a teacher was recently shot. In your school, different equals dead. So first things first, stay alive. You can make it. You're stronger than you give yourself credit for. And while you're surviving, don't for a second let yourself believe that those students' and teachers' assaults are deserved.

And here's why you can't give up: you will grow up to be STRONG and PROUD. You will kiss a boy one day (hell... you'll kiss a lot of boys). You'll fall in love and one day YOU WILL BE READY TO FIGHT BACK and you will FIGHT BACK HARD to help change this world so that no other child has to feel the way you do right now.

And guess what, that very High School you live in terror of today will invite you back as an honored guest. And on a sunny day in May your old school's entire student body will pack into the gymnasium to give you a standing ovation for having won an Academy Award for a gay liberation film. No, seriously, I'm not making this crap up.

And near the end of your speech that day, a young man very much like yourself will feel safe enough to stand up in front of his fellow students and come out of the closet. He'll get the second standing ovation of the day, so bring a tissue. And that "Health and Human Sexuality" teacher who condemns gay people, he still works there, but on this day he'll walk into that jam-packed, love filled auditorium, shake your hand and finally offer you the respect you deserve.

But for now, cry and howl and weep if you need to, because what they're doing to you IS wrong, it IS brutal, and tears are called for. And stay alive, work hard, consider the words you'll share with the world, but most of all -- let Jeremy from your swim team give you that first kiss. He's hot.

With admiration,

Dustin Lance Black

☆ my sweet moon,

It has taken me to reach age forty-three to finally feel ready to LIVE without adding any obstacles to my own path. If I could do it all again-to feel free sooner, to live more fully sooner-this is what I would say to you:

hummingbird
N
E — eagle   W — jaguar
S
serpent
dyslexia

* * *
Empathy
Drink more water
Eat more green veggies
Clean gut, clean head
Contemplate mountains & stars & TREES

"Watch your thoughts; they become words. Watch your words; they become actions. Watch your actions; they become habits. Watch your habits; they become character. Watch your character for it becomes your destiny."

(- the upanishads?
- The Tibetan Book of living & Dying?)

E.Q. over I.Q.   LAUGHTER over staying mad.

Take Piano lessons

It's ok to change your mind

Travel, cultivate kindness, temper your anger with nature & exercise, ask for help when you need it, look at peoples' actions as well as their words (if it walks & talks like a duck...) seek out yoga & yogic principles, take as many classes as you can that truly tug at your heart, leave if it feels like a time-waster and without apology, say no more, save your money & your energy for yourself & you really needed interests

♥Dance 5 rhythms
♥Sing
♥Play
♥Have a child

LOVE LOVE LOVE LOVE LOVE LOVE LOVE LOVE LOVE LOVE

Moon Unit Zappa

Joseph Galliano

Dear Me, A Letter to my 16-Year-Old Self

Twitter @JosephGalliano / @DearMeBook
www.josephgalliano.co.uk
www.dearme.org / dearmebooks.com
joseph@dearme.org

Dear Me,

It seems no time at all since I was you, yet you seem so distant.

You're overserious and overanxious—but sweet and well meaning; full of love and passion but also sadness and loss. Your skin doesn't fit you and you struggle to see your own qualities: your imagination and tastes are a boon, not a hindrance.

You are in some pain, but when you decide, it will stop. You'll be shocked by how happy you can be—but you need to make a decision to change. You do, but why not do it sooner? Happy is better than sad. And you DO get happy. It's better.

Even through the fog, I can see you better than you can, so here are a few pointers.

1. Sometimes it's okay to be first—you do deserve good stuff.
2. Up is sexier than down.
3. Life is not a puzzle; it's a game and it's not going on in the other room; it's wherever you are.
4. You are brilliant at getting what you want—so start wanting the good stuff.
5. Don't mourn Neil for so long—twenty-five years is too much. And after a while it becomes about you not him. He would want to be a happy memory, not a scar.
6. There is no such thing as cool—follow your enthusiasms honestly. The few records you ever bought to impress stay in their sleeves . . .
7. Except for the Stone Roses' first one. Ooooh lovely.
8. What job would you pay someone to let you do? Do that.

9. Pick up a guitar NOW . . . It's much more difficult when you lose that teenage obsessiveness.
10. Learn to say: "I've had enough to drink now, thank you." And don't start smoking—it's just nasty.
11. Get into the exercise habit—and team sport IS for boys like you.
12. In one year, when you see finally McCartney in concert (in rehearsal no less), don't grip his shoulder through his limo window and burble "thank you" in his face. It's not dignified and he won't thank you for it. He'll just look scared.
13. Forget all the above—don't change a thing. Be you: It's how you become me.

Cherish your siblings, all of them; cherish your parents; cherish your friends; be kinder to yourself; keep an eye out for Mark. Cherish him.

There's plenty more I could say, but you're probably itching to go thumb through that grubby secondhand record shop with Chris, so go on. Get me something I might still be listening to.

Call anytime

Joe—aged 39 (Editor and Journalist—YES . . . you read that right.)

P.S. In 23 years, when you finally sit down to write this letter, it will dawn on you why it has taken some people so long to do theirs and you'll be EVEN MORE grateful that they did!

Dear Me,

If, in future years, anyone asks you to give advice to your sixteen year old self...

don't.

Make your own unique messes, and then work your own way out of them.

See you,

Alan Rickman

Alan Rickman

SCIMITAR FILMS LTD.

Directors: Michael Winner MA (CANTAB), OBE (offered but rejected), John Fraser MA (OXON), M.Phil

219 KENSINGTON HIGH STREET
LONDON W8 6BD

Telephone 020 7734 8385
Fax 020 7602 9217
Email winner@ftech.co.uk

What I'd have written to myself when younger.

Success is not the swift of foot. It is to the person who perseveres, disregarding, or taking in his or her stride, the many setbacks, disappointments and rejections which will inevitably occur. You simply have to carry on. Being as self motivated and ingenious and above all as hard-working as you can. The world does not owe you a living. You have to go out and carve one for yourself. Jerome K Jerome wrote, "I like work: it fascinates me. I can sit and look at it for hours." I have few qualities but working hard is one of my attributes. I'd come in on Saturdays, Sundays, I'd work writing scripts, planning, plotting, until the late hours. Of all businesses, movies are the most grueling. After each film you are back on the out-of-work list. You can't wait for someone to phone sand offer you a job. You have to create scripts, create opportunities, cajole movie stars to have their name attached to your project. It is the perfect canvas. One which you can leave blank through sloth, inactivity or laziness, or one you can fill with activity and pleasure if you try hard enough. The old adage "If you don't succeed at first, try, try again" is as good as they come. Those who rise to it achieve something. Those who do not, those who fail to create opportunities or let opportunity pass them by are doomed to bitterness and failure. Or, to put it in simple English vernacular: take your finger out!

[signature: Michael Winner]

OFFICE: ABACUS HOUSE, 367 BLANDFORD ROAD, BECKENHAM, KENT BR3 4NW

S LTD.
W8 6BD

Royal Mail
11.04.11
London South
Mail Centre
08:15 pm
64007645

Please remember
to write the
postcode clearly

Dear Lynda,

You have an unwavering faith that you can and will achieve whatever you set as your life's goals. This confidence will serve you well. Never let a fear of failure hold you back from experiencing everything life has to offer.

You are blessed with many gifts, but for a successful, happy life, you need to be smart about your personal decisions. Live a life of integrity, listen to those you respect about choices you will make, and don't engage in reckless personal behaviors.

There is no benefit in worrying endlessly about pleasing everyone all the time. Do not spend your emotional energy on what is outside of your control.

At your age, life seems to stretch out endlessly, and you take your good health for granted. Know that life is a grand adventure and it goes by quickly. Seize the moments to live it well. Do the things you need to do to protect your health so you can enjoy life fully.

Your career is very important to you. To achieve much, hard work, commitment, and study are the prerequisites, and you must embrace those disciplines enthusiastically to succeed.

Never forget that however much you value your professional career, it is your personal life that will truly determine your happiness. So invest your time in your family and friends, and you will be rewarded many times over.

You alone are responsible for who you become and for your own happiness. You get back what you put into life, so always do your best—and remember, whatever happens, you are loved.

Love,

Lynda

Hey, Paul!

    Trust yourself, just like you're doing.

    Maybe lighten up.

    No. Don't lighten up.

    Here's what the kids say in the future:
No worries.
Same difference.
It's all good.

    Love & luck,
    Paul

While pondering this question I couldn't help but think of Ray Bradbury's great short story "A Sound of Thunder" that laid out the concept of the butterfly effect, which essentially posits that if even the slightest thing is altered in the past, the entire future of the world would come out differently. In Bradbury's imagination it went something like this; use a time machine to visit the prehistoric past, step on a butterfly, return to the present to find the Nazis won. Whoops.
So I think it probably would be a bad idea to tell myself in 1978 that on the night of Feb 19, 2000 I should stay at home, thereby avoiding meeting a person that would break my heart. I mean, who knows what that might lead to?

Rather I think I should stick to generalities that I think might be valuable to any 16 year old.
Be brave. Dont waste time comparing yourself to others, you are your own unique being and your path is your own. If you ever make any money handle it wisely. Don't start smoking, it's really hard to stop. If you live in California don't hang anything heavy or breakable over the bed, in an earthquake it will fall on you. Wear sunscreen every day and not just on your face, get all the parts that are hanging out of your clothes. Buckle up! Even when you are in back seat. Play well with others, often. Doesn't matter if it's golf, bridge, scrabble, ping pong, practical jokes...just keep playing. And singing loud and dancing, too. Be generous with your love, compliments, forgiveness, and hospitality. Always have animals in your life, just having a regularly filled bird feeder will bring you joy. And a dog? Pretty darn perfect.

Julie White

PAULY SHORE

Dear 16 year old Pauly Jr.,

If you knew everything that I know now, I'd probably tell you to kill yourself on your 17th birthday. Just end it all. You don't want to know what's coming. Kidding...

The main thing that you have to realize, Pauly Jr., is that when you go out into the real world, no one really cares about you. Of course, your friends and family do. But society and business don't. It's a weiz eat weiz world out there, and the quicker you realize that, the quicker you won't take things so seriously.

And, Pauly Jr., you know how you have a little vulnerable heart right now, and you look at the world with big, wide, baby eyes? Well, that's going to slowly change too. After getting screwed over three or four or five times by various women in relationships, you become a little bit numb. But, my advice to you is be OK with it. Numb is cool.

There will also be a time in your thirties when you become somewhat depressed. Experience it, feel it, and go with it. As far as your brothers and sister are concerned, those relationships are going to get somewhat awkward. But, then again, there are a lot of brothers and sisters that have awkward relationships when their parents get older.

Either way, my advice to you, 16 year old Pauly Jr., is just live in the moment and experience all the things that will be coming your way. Your MTV years are going to be a fucking blast. There will be a couple deaths of some very close personal friends, but just hang in there, you will get through it. And most importantly, just breathe and stick with your vision, which is bringing laughter to the world. Your legacy will live on for decades to come.

Goodbye young Jedi Pauly Jr. May the weiz be with you.

Sincerely,

Pauly Sr.

Dear Me,

It's junior year and things are as bad as ever. The so-called clique is filled with people who have nothing going for them except rich parents. People walk around so smug you'd think their noses were taped to the ceiling. The lies people had spread about you will continue to make you sick to your stomach. Senior year will be no better. Thank God or goddess or whoever you have for your small circle of friends who are as silly and fun as you can be. Stay in Shore Players, even though you can't really sing or act, so you don't have to go home and put up with more crap. You made the right decision to apply to the University of Georgia: You'll finally "find yourself." Even though you're clueless about what forestry school really entails. (You'll actually be up for forestry freshman of the year, even though you're considered the hippy of the forestry school because you wear horrible apple green polyester bell-bottoms from Sears and grew your hair longish.). Keep writing your humorous ideas down because eventually you'll take creative writing in journalism school and come up with poems that'll be the basis for your songs one day.

Fred Schneider III

**JERRY
SPRINGER**

Dear Gerald —

Do well in school —
learn as much as you can —
be nice to people — & don't
bother making plans as to
what you're going to be —
because you have little of any
control over it.

Life is a surprise. Just
be skilled, smart & prepared.

[signature]

Dear Me,

I've got a bit of advice for the coming years, kid. Please
at least consider these words throughout your life; believe
me, they'll come in handy when you least expect it.

I'll start it off on the subject of love and relationships.
You have a high tolerance for ignorance and stupidity
in people—because you're not necessarily looking for
anything from anyone—but I'll tell you this: You truly can
become those you're with. There are three types of people
in this place: those who love, those who hate, and those
who are stuck in between the two, like us.

Only let love into your life, don't waste your time with
hate, it's a useless emotion. If you need a gauge, use the
eyes and your gut. Follow nothing else. People's opinions
on the subject are meaningless. Everyone's experience is
different. Trust that the eyes will always betray deception.

On the subject of pleasure: God! I know you like to have
fun. Follow that joy until you overdose on it, just know that
the less you have of anything the more enjoyable it will be
when you finally get around to savoring it.

As far as conflict goes, you're going to see more of it than most people, largely because you question everything in life. Don't ever change that; just know that when conflict arises, your love is your gun, kid.

Nothing murders hatred quicker than joy. Your genuine laughter and understanding that nothing in life matters more than good people, love, and following your joy will kill any evil obstacle in your path.

Believe me, karma exists. Fighting and seeking vengeance is futile. Don't bother. When someone who hates you sees your clean spirit, full of joy and laughter, you've already defeated them. Your joy will annihilate all haters with envy. It doesn't matter how much money, power—or stuff—you have in life, joy is the ultimate goal for most humans.

Ah, yes . . . procrastination is one of your biggest issues in life, kid. Do me a favor, when you think it, do it. I know you like to envision everything in your mind as completed and this process makes you bored at the thought of actually finishing anything. I'll tell you now that when I look back, I see nothing but what's been done. Life is composed of journeys and accomplishments: Yes, dream, but then you need to manifest that dream immediately.

What are you waiting for?

Last but not least, I'm going to inform you that the most satisfying endeavors in life consist of you using your fear as a conquering weapon against obstacles. If you fear it, run toward it like a train, kid. Life is short, and if humans have multiple lives, the best way to assure you will evolve your soul efficiently in every lifetime is to follow your fears and conquer them. They are obstacles between your soul and the next plateau after Earth.

I Love You,

Michelle Rodriguez from the future

P.S. Stop being such a prude about sex too—you may dismiss your husband one day by being too careful.

Dear Self,   May 1, 2011 (can you believe it!)

First of all, if you are reading this it means that time travel is possible. Go immediately to Cambridge University, and find a man named Stephen Hawking and tell him about it. If he doubts you, tell him that the Berlin wall will fall in Oct. 1989. He 'll call you back eventually. Next, right now you and everyone around you is worrying that the world is going to end in a nuclear apocalypse. Don't worry about it. Not going to happen. Also If you find the time, put a few dollars into a company called Microsoft. If you don't get around to it, don't sweat it. It's no big deal.

Lastly, know this. You are worthy of love, just the way you are. Think of a new born child, who screams all night, and does all sorts of nasty, stinking things to it's Parents and still is constantly lovable. You are no different, just a bit older. This is true for everyone. The world may try to convince you otherwise. The world will be mistaken. Love yourself every day. You are worth it.

Much respect,

James Marsters

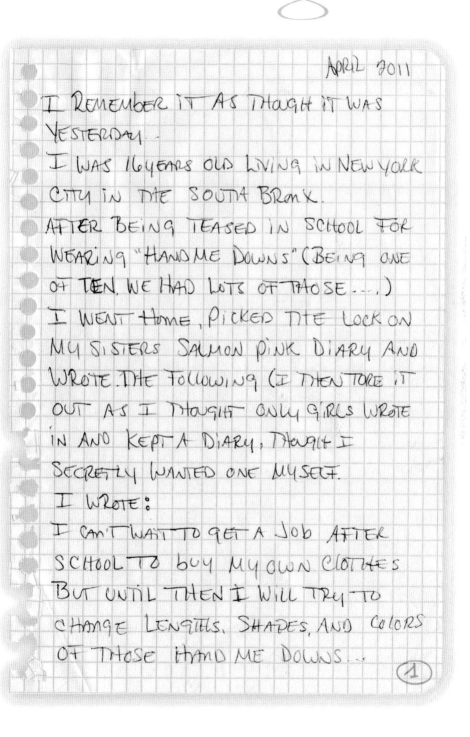

APRIL 2011

I REMEMBER IT AS THOUGH IT WAS
YESTERDAY.

I WAS 16 YEARS OLD LIVING IN NEW YORK
CITY IN THE SOUTH BRONX.

AFTER BEING TEASED IN SCHOOL FOR
WEARING "HAND ME DOWNS" (BEING ONE
OF TEN, WE HAD LOTS OF THOSE....)

I WENT HOME, PICKED THE LOCK ON
MY SISTERS SALMON PINK DIARY AND
WROTE THE FOLLOWING (I THEN TORE IT
OUT AS I THOUGHT ONLY GIRLS WROTE
IN AND KEPT A DIARY, THOUGH I
SECRETLY WANTED ONE MYSELF.

I WROTE:

I CAN'T WAIT TO GET A JOB AFTER
SCHOOL TO BUY MY OWN CLOTHES
BUT UNTIL THEN I WILL TRY TO
CHANGE LENGTHS, SHADES, AND COLORS
OF THOSE HAND ME DOWNS...

①

SO THAT THEY ALWAYS LOOK
DIFFERENT AND THEY CAN NEVER
MAKE FUN OF ME AGAIN FOR
WEARING THE SAME CLOTHES THAT
MY BROTHER WORE.
EVEN THOUGH FUN WAS MADE OF ME
LATER IN LIFE FOR OTHER REASONS
WHICH PAID OFF... HAHAHA...!
LITTLE DID I KNOW IT PREPARED ME
CREATIVELY FOR LIFE, AND TO THIS
VERY DAY I STILL CHANGE LENGTHS
SHAPES, AND COLORS OF CLOTHES THAT
ARE GIVEN TO ME NOW. NOT BY MY
BROTHERS. BUT BY DESIGNERS AND
DESIGNER FRIENDS, AND NOW AT 6FT4,
37 INSEAM, AND A WAIST LINE THAT
CHANGES WITH THE CITY I'M IN...
I'M ALWAYS DOING SOMETHING TO
MAKE SOME OF THE CLOTHES WORK.

②

I NOW LOOK BACK AND THANK THOSE
KIDS THEY DID NOT KNOW THAT BY
TEASING ME THEY GAVE ME POWER
AND UNLEASHED MY CREATIVITY TO
MATCH MY "FAGULOUS" PERSONALITY
AND CHARACTER ON VERY LITTLE OR
NO BUDGET.

AND THAT PINK BOOK (DIARY)
I MENTIONED EARLIER THAT I SO
SECRETLY WANTED.
WELL NOW I CAN GET IT IN MANY
COLOR'S AND DON'T HAVE TO PICK THE LOCK,
TEAR OUT THE PAGE, OR CARE ABOUT
BEING TEASED AS I USE ONE
EVERYDAY AND ITS CALLED
AN "AGENDA"...

J. Alexander
AKA "Miss J"

(3)

At sixteen my Dads Gone, I have to try to be the head of the family. I seem to fall in love easily and deeply.

WHEN I WAS 16

Dear Me,

It's a problem. I love music and Jazz is happening all around me, but I also love films. That would be a dream come true to be in films.

I'm not a person who looks like a star; will I be a good enough actor. My work lets me play in front of different Audiences and I try to figure out if sometimes when I stop the show. Is it the classical playing or my love of Victor Borge, his humor I use to make fun of the serious way that classical people see themselves. I have to come to a decision. Am I going to be an incredible violinist and obey that discipline or see my teachers and explain my dreams to them?

I know I'm young. I need to study electronics and play all kinds of music and be ready when the opportunity comes. I don't want my Mom to be disappointed after all the sacrifices she has made for my sister and me. Will she support these youthful dreams? I now have a small job after school and am being mentored in musical engineering. I am an intern. Will I perform more frequently and love it? I got variety and humor. My friends are musicians and actors. I'm lucky and I am thankful for the chance. I hope I don't screw up.

PHIL RAMONE

Phil Ramone

MARCH 19TH

DEAR NEIL —

CONGRATULATIONS ON MAKING IT THIS FAR! NOT EVERYONE DOES, SO GOOD JOB ON THAT. YOU'VE GOT A LONG WAYS TO GO BUT HEY, IT'S A START...

NOT TO SPOIL THE PARTY OR ANYTHING, BUT HERE'S THE BAD NEWS: YOU ARE GOING TO FAIL. MANY TIMES. FAR MORE OFTEN THAN YOU WILL SUCCEED AND IN WAYS BOTH LARGE AND SMALL. NOT ALL PEOPLE WILL NOTICE OR CARE, BUT YOU'LL BE THERE TO FEEL EACH ONE OF THEM. IT WILL HURT, TIME AFTER TIME, AND SOME FAILURES YOU WILL MAKE MORE THAN ONCE — IT DOESN'T MATTER, IT HAPPENS, KEEP GOING. IT'S WORTH IT. LIFE ENDS UP BEING WORTH IT.

I KNOW THAT YOU WILL EVENTUALLY LOVE YOUR WORK — DON'T MAKE THE MISTAKE OF LOVING IT MORE THAN THE PEOPLE AROUND YOU. IF YOU DO THEN IT WILL BE A DISASTER, I PROMISE. IF YOU CAN, GO BACK AND FIX IT. IMMEDIATELY. NO MATTER HOW LONG IT TAKES.

I KNOW THAT AT YOUR AGE YOU FEEL IMMORTAL BUT YOU'RE NOT. THE CLOCK IS TICKING, SO HAVE SOME FUN, DO GOOD THINGS AND DO THEM TODAY. TOMORROW MAY BE TOO LATE.

WITH LOVE,
Neil

* I ALMOST FORGOT: HAPPY BIRTHDAY!

Ricki Lake

May 2011

Dearest Ricki (Earlier, 1984 Model),

I know it's not easy being an awkward, chubby teenager with the gift of gab; believe me, I've been there. In your heart, you know you're destined to connect with people by sharing your life experiences – already marked by both wonderful memories and dark parts of the past – but your exterior doesn't match the confident entertainer who is waiting to relate to the world.

Continue to cultivate your love of the arts and communication; keep performing and honing your skills on every small stage in Manhattan, standing in the face of your insecurities. Discuss your ideas and your perspectives with your family and friends. In fact, don't hold back at all. Engage with those around you. Tell your story.

There will always be people who try to lower your voice. Some won't think you have the talent or looks to "succeed." Others will attempt to change your path. You should listen – because a true communicator is present and involved – but, don't hear them. Let those folks spark your competitive nature, and follow your heart. Drown out the doubts by talking louder.

Talking is good. In fact, it turns out to be your future and your fortune. There are two talk shows, three books, more than a dozen feature films and a few TV series waiting for you – so speak up, and continue to be heard. Someday soon, the world is going to be listening!

With love,

Ricki (All-New, 2011 Model)

Dear Alan,

First of all, you're right. You're right about who you think is wrong. You're right to trust your instincts and to be your own person.

Second of all, slow down. Before you know it you'll be away from home and you'll be living your own life. Don't waste energy trying to make time move faster, because it won't until one day when you don't want it to and you'll wonder if all those nights spent longing for the future are now being paid back by making a beautiful present more fleeting. So please, if only for my karmic peace of mind, chill out about it, ok?

You're going to be really, really happy one day and you're going to have a life that is so far from your comprehension right now that I'm not even going to try to explain how it happens. I can hardly work it out myself. You just have to go with the flow, Alan. Just let go and tumble through life. It will all be okay.

But it's not a commercial. There are really shitty bits. You don't even know it but right now there are things happening to you that are too painful to process and so, like the adults around you, you're just not dealing with them, suppressing them, locking them up in a box in your mind. When you're 28, that box is going to explode open and tear your life apart. Everything will change and there will be much pain and it will take you a long time to recover. But recover you will, and it will ultimately make you a better person, and those you love will benefit too.

You're going to have lots of sex and you're going to feel sexy. Don't worry. Just try and remember that it's better for you to feel sexy about yourself than for other people to tell you you are. It's going to be okay.

In 1997 you'll meet someone in New York at the party for the opening night of 'Titanic - the Musical'. Now, I am not one for regrets, Alan, and I truly believe that everything you experience between 16 and now all contributes to make you the really happy person that you become, so how could I wish any of it to be different? But, come on, the show is called 'Titanic', that should be an omen. Walk away from this person. You'll never make them not be angry. Later on you'll see a pattern of you trying to fix angry people and you'll be able to break it, so do yourself a favour and walk away, let this one be the first. He will try to destroy you. He won't, but he'll try very hard.

You will love and be loved and be rich beyond your wildest dreams, and the best thing about this richness is that it has nothing to do with money. It's all going to be okay.

A teacher at drama school is going to tell you that you'll never make it as a professional actor. He is wrong. Wrong to say it, and just wrong because you do okay. Try not to let it dent you too much.

You're never going to have children, Alan. You're going to try, in relationships with both women and men, but it doesn't happen, and that's okay too. Right now you have the happiest family anyone could wish for.

It really is all going to be okay. I'll see you in 29 years. Enjoy it.

Love from Alan x

William Shatner

April 2011

Dear Billy:

I'm sure I catch you harried, tense, and nervous about the girl next to you upon whose body you'd like to jump. I know your hormones are raging and you hide your erection so no one can see by pressing your school books against your lap and trying to think of mother and baby.

If you are not thinking about girls, then you are thinking about football. Yes, I thought you could run fast enough, throw far enough, and survive the head pounding blows by defensive players 100 pounds heavier than you. Was I mistaken? Did Haskel Blaur run faster than you and beat you out of the running back position? I know he did. Whatever became of Haskel?

Perhaps you're thinking of the tiny stage at Victoria Park and the play that Violet Walters wants to put on and whether you are adequate or not.

Yes, that inadequacy. It's there all the time, isn't it? Can you remember your lines? Will you faint in front of the audience? Will you step off the stage into oblivion? Can you run as fast as Haskel Blaur? Will that girl ever put her arms around you and tell you that she loves you? Come to think of it, wouldn't it be great if Daddy and Mummy said that they loved you? Wait – maybe they did in their own way. It's hard to figure, isn't it?

Well, let me tell you, it all works out. The girl finally tells you she loves you, the stage awaits you and is your forum, and I'm sorry, but football is not your calling.

My word of advice to you my son, my boy, is to live in the moment. Enjoy those feelings of inadequacy, succumb to the terror of your hormonal disorder, live in your youth, because it passes too quickly. What will be, will be, and although there is much you can do about it, in the end, there isn't much you can do about it. The idea is to keep trying. Don't let up. Things happen - good, bad, dull and exciting. Survive, struggle and keep the love in your heart. The truism of one life to live is there because that's true. Enjoy the music of your life because once the band stops playing, that's it.

With great love,

Bill Shatner (in case you didn't know)

Bill

From: **Jimmy Wales**
To: **Jimmy age 16**
Subject: **Dear Me**

Boo! Did I scare you? I'm you, from the future. I have lived the life that you—that we, you and I, me—chose. We did all right for the most part, but we did screw up here and there. Since I have this opportunity to write to you, I have a couple of suggestions. Trust me, I know, I've been there. I've been you. I am you.

You're a bright guy, but you don't always trust your instincts. Go for it.

Every time you've doubted yourself and failed to act, you've seen later that you were right and could have gotten to where you got eventually, much sooner. Every time you were overconfident and made a misstep, and seen later that you were wrong . . . well, you know what? You just learned from it and grew stronger.

Don't self-censor. When you have an idea, implement it. Don't wait until you're sure so that you won't have a failure. Instead, fail faster.

—Jimmy

HEY, LADY,

YES, YOU LANKY LEAN PERSON IN AN ULTRASUEDE MIDI-COAT.

WHERE ARE YOU RUSHING OFF TO? DOWN THE HALLWAYS OF SAGUARO HIGH SCHOOL IN SCOTTSDALE, ARIZONA, AVOIDING THE KIDS WHO JUST DON'T GET IT? I UNDERSTAND AND I DON'T BLAME YOU. BUT SOMEDAY THEY WILL AND THEN IT WON'T MATTER.

YOU ARE REALLY SOMETHING IN A SHAG HAIRCUT AND BELL-BOTTOM JEANS. A LIVE WIRE, A SPARK READY TO IGNITE. FILLED WITH DREAMS AND FANTASIES AND ENDLESS EXCITEMENT AT THE THOUGHT OF ALL THAT THE FUTURE HOLDS. SITTING IN YOUR ROOM, DECORATED WITH ASTROLOGICAL WALLPAPER, BLACK LIGHT POSTERS, YOUR OWN STEREO, WHERE YOU SIT ON YOUR INDIAN BEDSPREAD LISTENING TO JONI MITCHELL *LADIES OF THE CANYON* AND CAROLE KING *TAPESTRY* AND CAT STEVENS, THERE YOU ARE WALKING ON A MOON SHADOW, THE DESERT OUTSIDE YOUR WINDOW, AND A THOUSAND JOURNEYS AWAIT.

YOU LONG FOR INDEPENDENCE AND APPLAUSE, LOVE AND CELEBRATION.

PATIENCE, MY DEAR SANDY, THAT IS THE KEY TO HAPPINESS.

SITTING QUIETLY AND KNOWING ALL GOOD THINGS ARE ON THEIR WAY.

IT APPEARS AT TIMES THAT THEY AREN'T, BUT IT'S JUST A TEST OF YOUR OWN INNER EMERGENCY BROADCAST SYSTEM.

Letter to my sixteen-year-old self

Dear Rob,

So glad to have this opportunity to write to you. So much has changed since we were sixteen. I thought maybe if I got you this letter, you could use it here and there to help you out. Though I know that you probably won't. First, know that I'm writing this to you as I'm about to turn forty, so that whole thing about dying before you were twenty-one was really just a misguided romantic notion and you're better off that it's not true. That said:

1. I know your mom drives you crazy, but she won't be here forever, so try to appreciate your time with her.
2. Don't worry when your heart gets broken, you meet an amazing woman who will change your life. You'll know her when you meet her.
3. Try to stop smoking now.
4. Those pants are a bad idea.
5. No matter how many people try to tell you how great the odds are against you finding a future in the music business, please keep at it. It works out for you.
6. You won't go blind if you play with it too much.
7. There will be a day when every time someone told

you "enjoy your youth" will echo in your head. Try to do it now. It really is special.

8. You're spending a lot of time trying to figure out who you want to be. In the end, you will be you. It will feel good and bad. You will feel cool and like a fool, but all in all, you will be glad for all of the idiosyncrasies that make up who you are.

There's a lot more, but anything else may spoil the ride. The only thing I will tell you is that even now, I don't have it all figured out. I know we thought I would, but somehow that's what makes me at this age sometimes feel like me at your age. Good luck.

Rt

Letter to My Sixteen Year Old Self
(from my thirteen year old self)

Dear Zachary,

I imagine at 16, you're driving that Volvo, your choice of a first car because of its safety record.

You've probably completed the script you began at age 13 in hopes of becoming a writer/director some day.

Have you starred in an action film like Indiana Jones or worked with Steven Spielberg or Leonardo DiCaprio.

Did you eat enough vegetables and drink enough milk to get to be 6' tall?

I'm sure you have accomplished some of your dreams by now. You have your whole life ahead of you to make a difference. Hold onto your dreams and just keep believing!

Zach

MEDECINS SANS FRONTIERES
DOCTORS WITHOUT BORDERS

Dear 16-year-old Froggy,

You looked so happy and pretty in that dress the other night. Did you see it? You and your friend Tim leading your friends down the road at graduation? What an honor it is to be a part of some of your best friends' magical moment.

I sense that you didn't see how beautiful you were. Your friends and family really love you just the way you are, whether you bleach your hair blonde or are flat chested.

Your love of adventure and unique talents are so amazing and inspirational!
At this moment you are set on becoming maybe a ski instructor or doing something with kids. You are really not sure what you want to do but guess what? You are going to go to college, design your own major and work as a recreational therapist for kids in trouble! You will go to California and fall in love with the west coast! And at 27 you will go to nursing school work at a great hospital called Long Beach Memorial and one day (after doing short term medical trips to Guatemala) say goodbye to California and hello to a life beyond your wildest dreams!

Don't be discouraged by the application for a job at Doctors without Borders! Just go for it! Your first adventure will take you to Sri Lanka (you had to ask where that was!) to a surgical program in a very isolated war-torn part of the country. You will have the friends that you meet there for life, and they will show up when you need them the most.

You will get in some hairy situations, learn to cry, laugh and have fun. You will learn how people endure suffering and still show up to work to teach you about how to care for people. For example, you will get very sick with Malaria in Sierra Leone and your friend and co-worker John will help you get the treatment you need. You will be in an isolation unit in Angola taking care of the deadly disease Marburg and will continue to take care of persons with an incurable disease....but Maria and her mom walked out of the hospital! Why??? Because you and your team believed they would and you never gave up.

You will hike the hills of Kashmir after the earthquake looking for ill children and severely injured people that could not make it to your tent! That was amazing! You and your team will help provide some dignity and nutrition for all those young men and women in prison in Zimbabwe.

You will meet people from all over the world: Yolanda, Mohammed, John, Simba, Blessing, Vera, Alli and hundreds more who will show you how to live a life you could never imagine.

You will walk for miles in Haiti meeting amazing people under bed sheets and fighting one disaster after another. You will stand and watch helplessly as children die in front of you. You will initially feel anger and frustration of how people are not doing things *like you think they should* but you will see that when you learn some acceptance and appreciation for cultural differences you will totally get it.

You will sleep in clay huts, tents and houses in the communities you are working in. You will dress fully like a Muslim woman and you will eat and drink soup out of a shared bowl while sitting on the floor in the mosque in Tajikistan.

You will have an incident (or two) that will be life shattering and will totally wake you up to what is important in your life… family, friends and a life with purpose.

You will soon find out that the world welcomes you and all you have to give….

Wow! As I write this, two dolphins have just swum by this deserted beach - just to check in and send you/me their love from the sea!

All you have to do is to reach out and touch the magic that surrounds you and be yourself. Keep scanning the horizon for adventures, keep testing the upper limits of your physical world and hang on for the ride of your life! Keep enjoying the skiing, the horseback riding and team sports.

You will hit some speed bumps along the way: The "I am not good enough/ pretty enough/ smart enough/ etc" years will be dark and lonely, but I will always be here for you, keeping the light on to let you know that I love you, like the dolphins in front of you now joyously playing and surfing the waves…

'till we meet again

Your inspired self

Mary Jo Frawley

Froggy (Ageless)
MSF Aid Worker

If you enjoyed reading the letters here, why not write your own?

Use the following pages to compose a letter to yourself at sixteen, scan it, and email it to us—with a picture of yourself at around that age if you can—or simply send it as an email to myletter@dearme.org. We can then post it on our blog at dearmebooks.com.

Or you can find us at Twitter on @DearMeBook—add us and why not #tweetyour16yearoldself?

Read your letter into a video camera and post your films to our YouTube channel, youtube.com/dear16yearoldme, and check out other videos there.

Come and interact on our Facebook page, facebook.com/DearMeBooks, and also check out dearme.org.

We couldn't have done any of that when we were sixteen years old. Enjoy!

ACKNOWLEDGMENTS
Dear You . . .
With Thanks To . . .

The editor wishes to send a huge thank-you to all the contributors: you have been generous with your time, hearts, and imaginations.

Ultraspecial thanks to J. K. Rowling for giving us some of her special magic, and to Peter Kay for so generously approaching his friend on our behalf.

Everyone at Atria Books, particularly Judith Curr, Peter Borland, Nick Simonds, Isolde Sauer, Kyoko Watanabe, Dana Sloan, Jim Thiel, Fausto Bozza, and Paul Olsewski; and all at Simon & Schuster UK, especially Mike Jones, Nigel Stoneman, Colin Midson, and Ally Glynn.

My agent Charlotte Robertson at Aitken Alexander Associates for her guidance, enthusiasm, and belief.

Extraspecial thanks to Christopher Racster; Moon Zappa; Sarah, the Duchess of York; Beverly D'Angelo; and Greg Gorman for going above and beyond.

Letters of commendation and gratitude to everyone who has given of their time, help, and support in so many different ways, with apologies for the inevitable startling omissions.

Aaron Kanter, Adam Peck, Al Mobbs, Alan Nierob, Aleen

Keshishian, Alexandra J. Heller, Alisa Walters, Alison Barrow, Alison Owen, Andrew Davis, Andrew Onraet, Andy at Costa Communications, Andy Serkis, Anna Makowka, Beth Bourgeois, Betsy Hackman, Brenda Feldman, Calum Brannan, Camilla Young, Cat Clausi, Catherine Shepherd, Celia Walden, Cherry Hepburn, Chris Black, Clair Dobbs, Claire Comiskey, Craig Axtell, Craig Schneider, Cynthia Snyder, Dan Bodansky, Dan Scheinkman, David Drury, David López, Doug MacLaren, Ed Carlo Pisapia, Erika Thomas, Evan Weiss, Florence Avery, Gal Uchovsky, George Prior, Giacomo Palazo, Giulia Melucci, Henry Medina, Hugh Wright, Ian Jeanes, Jack Beck, James Henderson, Jamie Huckbody, Jason Weinberg, Jay Walsh, Jeff Abraham, Jennifer Crawford, Jennifer Tierney, Jerry Schmidt, Jocelyn Whinney, Joe Phelan, Jon Lys Turner, Josh Sabarra, Judy Katz, Juliet Dawson, Julio Cano Murcia, Justin Bond, Kathleen Hays, Kathy Travis, Ken Christiansan, Kenneth Hartung, Kerry Hood, Kevin Carr, Kristina Sorenson, Laura Ackermann, Leah Middleton, Libby Caudwell, Libby Caufield, Lillian LaSalle, Linda Shafran, Lisa Power, Liz Mendez, Lizzie Balloon, Lori Jo Tanaka, Maddi Bonura, Marcel Pariseau, Marielle Abuanza, Mark Hutchinson, Mark King, Mark Palmer-Edgecumbe, Matthew Dunning, Merritt Blake, Michelle Lederer, Mike Anderson, Mike Kelly, Mike Phifer, Mitchell Gossett, Moira Bellas, Nancy Seltzer, Natalie Wright, Nathan Smith, Nicole Perez-Krueger, Nikola Barisic, Olivier Sultan, Paige Glaves, Paul Dawson, Paul Levatino, Pete Sanders, PJ DeBoy, Rachel McCormack, Rachel Virden, Rachel Waterman, Ray Marks, Rebecca Salt, Rich Dawes, Rob Tokar, Robyn Watson, Ron Hoffman, Rupert Fowler, Sally Bowles, Sally Howard, Sara Switzer, Sarah Owen, Sean Katz, Simon and Tanis Raccioppa, Stephen Bender, Stephen Figge, Steve Himber, Steve Lau, Steve Nguyen, Stuart Bell, Stuart Watts, Sue Brearley, Sue Cameron, Sue Harris, Sue Madore, Susan

Allenback, Tim Harms, Tim Pinckney, Toby Mamis, Tom Robinson, Topher Larkin, Tracey Chapman, Tyler Pietz, and Zack Morgenroth.

Polly, Roger, Catherine, and James O'Neil; Sophia and Danny Austin; Mark, Melanie, Jack, and Harry Galliano; and, most of all, Mark Doig, without whom . . .

Thank you.

MÉDECINS SANS FRONTIÈRES
DOCTORS WITHOUT BORDERS

DOCTORS WITHOUT BORDERS/ MÉDECINS SANS FRONTIÈRES

Doctors Without Borders/Médecins Sans Frontières (MSF) is an international medical humanitarian organization created by doctors and journalists in France in 1971.

Today, MSF provides aid in nearly seventy countries to people whose survival is threatened by violence, neglect, or catastrophe, primarily due to armed conflict, epidemics, malnutrition, exclusion from health care, or natural disasters. Based on the humanitarian principles of medical ethics and impartiality, MSF's work provides independent, impartial assistance to those most in need.

As an organization, MSF is neutral. MSF does not take sides in armed conflicts, provides care on the basis of need alone, and pushes for increased independent access to victims of conflict as required under international humanitarian law. MSF often speaks out to bring attention to neglected crises, to challenge inadequacies or abuse of the aid system, and to advocate for improved medical treatments and protocols. The organization is committed to bringing quality medical care to people in crisis regardless of their race, religion, or political affiliation and operates independently of any political, military, or religious agendas. One key to MSF's ability to act independently in response to a crisis is its independent funding. Ninety percent of MSF's overall funding comes from private, nongovernmental sources.

Some of MSF's recent work includes treating 1.1 million people for malaria—predominately in Africa, conducting 16,500 surgeries for people impacted by the Haiti earthquake, and treating more than 190,000 people living with HIV/AIDS around the world.

In 1999, MSF received the Nobel Peace Prize.

To learn more, visit doctorswithoutborders.org.